Organized and Engaged

Simple and Effective Strategies to Support Executive Function

Julie Tourigny, OTD, MS, OTR/L

Gryphon House
www.gryphonhouse.com

Copyright

Published by Gryphon House, Inc.
P. O. Box 10, Lewisville, NC 27023
800.638.0928; 877.638.7576 [fax]
Visit us on the web at www.gryphonhouse.com.

Library of Congress Control Number: 2023945474

Bulk Purchase

Gryphon House books are available for special premiums and sales promotions as well as for fund-raising use. Special editions or book excerpts also can be created to specifications. For details, call 800.638.0928.

Disclaimer

Gryphon House, Inc., cannot be held responsible for damage, mishap, or injury incurred during the use of or because of activities in this book. Appropriate and reasonable caution and adult supervision of children involved in activities and corresponding to the age and capability of each child involved are recommended at all times. Do not leave children unattended at any time. Observe safety and caution at all times.

Table of Contents

Introduction

Hello, early childhood educators!

Do you have children in your classroom who have difficulty remembering the rules, gathering their materials independently, or completing activities in a timely manner? Do you work with children who find it hard to follow and remember instructions so they can complete activities on their own? These children may be struggling with executive function.

The brain is remarkable. It is able to store almost infinite amounts of information, draw upon this information when needed, attend to what is important while simultaneously filtering out all of the unimportant things going on, and develop and achieve goals (Anderson et al., 2001). This is executive function. Executive function helps people remember what they need to, attend to what they are supposed to, and maintain control over their thoughts and actions so they can be successful in planning, completing, and executing goal-driven activities (Anderson, 2002). Children rely on executive-function skills to learn, play, and socialize throughout the school day.

In the classroom, executive function is responsible for helping children to:

- generate words and ideas,
- switch gears when something disrupts the usual routine,
- socialize and get along with peers,
- follow and remember multistep directions in the correct sequence,
- sustain attention to start and finish projects,
- problem solve, and
- regulate their emotions and behaviors.

Children use executive-function skills when they set a goal, plan steps to reach it, and sustain attention to achieve it. The stronger the executive-function skills, the more successful children will be at learning and socializing.

Children with emerging or poorly developed executive-function skills may struggle in the classroom with sustained attention, impulse control, time management, problem solving, and social interactions. Difficulties with executive function affect children's ability to remember information, multitask, plan and organize, and attend to what they should (Michel and Bimmüller, 2023; Stahl and Pry, 2005; van der Veer, Cantell, Minnaert, and Houwen, 2022). These children may lag behind their peers, abandon projects without finishing them, struggle with friendships, or have difficulty consistently following the rules and routines of the classroom. Consider the following two scenarios.

> During circle time, Liam sits quietly alongside his classmates and listens to his teacher, Mr. Jeffries, describe the seated activity the class will work on when circle time ends. After he's finished explaining the steps children will engage in to complete the activity, Mr. Jeffries dismisses the class to their seats. Liam quietly transitions to his seat and sits down. While the other children begin to work on the activity, Liam does not. Instead, he fiddles with his pencil while staring off into space. When Mr. Jeffries approaches him, Liam tells him that he's not sure what he's supposed to be doing. Mr. Jeffries reminds him of the activity and the steps he described earlier. Liam nods his head but still struggles to start working.

> Jayden, a six-year-old kindergartner, always seems to be a step behind his classmates. He often starts his classwork but never finishes it. His desk is disorganized, and he seldom knows where his materials are. One afternoon, his classroom teacher keeps him inside at recess so he can organize his desk. Instead of tidying it up, Jayden sits at his desk fiddling with a pen. When his teacher asks him if he needs help, Jayden asks earnestly, "With what?" His teacher gently replies, "To get your desk cleaned up so you can find what you need when you need to." Jayden shrugs and says, "It's not that bad. I know where everything is."

Jayden struggles with problem-solving and task completion. He also does not realize that having a neat and organized desk might help him work more efficiently. Liam's difficulty with executive function affects his focus and attention, ability to remember and follow directions, and goal-directed behavior.

The good news for Jayden and Liam is that there are many simple yet effective strategies to teach, improve, and support executive-function skills. This book describes these cognitive, behavioral, and sensory strategies; explains when to implement them; and describes how to create an environment that supports all children as they navigate learning, working memory, time management, problem-solving, and impulse control throughout the school day.

How to Use This Book

In a classroom environment that supports executive function, children are better at flexible thinking, self-control, remembering what they need to, and paying attention to what they are supposed to. Children with strong executive-function skills are better at problem-solving, socializing, and completing schoolwork successfully.

Chapter one describes in depth what executive-function skills are. Chapter two defines the important skill of self-regulation and explains how it supports executive functioning. Chapters three through six describe specific sensory, play, and cognitive strategies educators can implement to teach, nurture, and support student's executive functions. Finally, chapter seven explains how to use the strategies described in the previous chapters to support executive functioning throughout the day.

Refer to *Organized and Engaged* often for ideas to help support:

- Flexible thinking
- Transitioning from one activity to the next
- Remaining calm when something disrupts the usual routine

- Social interactions
- Problem solving
- Time management and completing activities in a timely manner
- Sustained attention and focus
- Self-control

Organized and Engaged offers many strategies, activities, and suggestions to help all children develop strong executive-function skills that they can rely on throughout the day as they navigate social interactions, new learning material, and unexpected changes and disruptions.

Let's get started!

Chapter 1:

Executive Function: What It Is and Why It Matters

Executive function is a group of mental skills that includes attentional flexibility, working memory, and inhibitory control. Children rely on these three executive-function skills to learn, play, and socialize throughout the school day as they:

- make transitions,
- take turns,
- learn to understand other people's points of view,
- practice self-control,
- problem solve,
- complete activities in a timely manner,
- remain on task,
- socialize with peers, and
- negotiate conflict.

For example, consider the skills required of children as they transition from home to the classroom. During this time, children participate in an established classroom routine as they remember to place their things in their cubbies, sign in, and wash their hands. Once these steps are complete, they must find something appropriate to engage with that will occupy their time while they wait for class to begin.

Children also utilize their executive-function skills in more complex ways. For example, when children sit still during circle time, they must listen to their teacher while blocking out the unnecessary sights and sounds happening all around them. They have to keep their hands to themselves and refrain from socializing with their peers. Then, they must sustain their attention for the duration of the time. If the teacher gives instructions for the next activity, children must remember what they were just told as they transition to their seats, gather the materials they need to complete the activity, and start working.

People are not born with executive functions. These skills develop and improve with time and practice. From preschool through first grade, children's executive-function abilities improve exponentially as they grow and mature (Michel and Bimmüller, 2023; Montroy et al., 2016). Some children quickly develop strong executive-function skills, while others struggle. The encouraging news is that it is possible to improve the executive functions of struggling children by employing simple yet effective classroom strategies and supports throughout the school day. When attentional flexibility, working memory, and inhibitory control are practiced and talked about in the school setting, everyone benefits.

To improve executive-function skills in the classroom, it is important to understand the three components of executive function:

- Attentional flexibility
- Working memory
- Inhibitory control

Attentional Flexibility

Attentional flexibility is the ability to switch focus from one person, task, or activity to another in response to a change in the situation. Children with age-appropriate attentional flexibility are able to pay attention to whom or what they are supposed to, while ignoring the irrelevant visual and auditory information around them. They can remain flexible when something, such as a fire alarm, a spilled drink, or an abrupt change to the routine, requires them to shift their attention to something else.

Children with strong attentional flexibility skills are better at paying attention to what they are supposed to, filtering out distractions, reacting well to disruptions to the normal routine, playing in new ways, and problem solving.

Of course, rules and routines are important in all early childhood classrooms, but disruptions are inevitable. Children need to be able to adapt to unexpected changes to the usual routine, for example, when it's too cold to go outside and recess must happen indoors, a good friend is absent from school, a favorite toy is missing, or a classmate changes the way they play a game.

> Alonzo arrives at preschool only to find that his three best friends are absent. Each morning, the four of them play together cooperatively in the building and construction center. Alonzo enters this space and tries to play on his own but realizes it isn't as fun without his friends. He looks around the room and sees other children playing at the sensory table. He joins the group and begins to mix, scoop, and pour, clearly enjoying his time.

Alonzo demonstrates good attentional flexibility when he switches gears and plays with a different group of children in a different area of the classroom with no difficulty. Attentional flexibility is responsible for filtering, task switching, and flexible thinking.

Filtering

Filtering is the ability to recognize the difference between important and irrelevant information. This allows children to filter out incoming information that is not important to them. In the classroom setting, these are typically visual and auditory distractions, such as a people passing by in the hallway, conversations the child isn't part of, activities going on outside that the child might observe through a window, fans spinning, or heaters clicking on and off. Not only does the brain need to filter out this extraneous information, but it must also remain alert to incoming information that may be important, such as a fire alarm or a surprise visitor to the classroom.

Children who struggle with filtering may have difficulty concentrating in a noisy classroom. They may experience fatigue or give up on an activity because it is hard for them to focus on one thing. Instead, they expend mental energy focusing on everything at once: the visual distractions, sounds and conversations occurring throughout the classroom, and the activity they should be working on.

Task Switching

Task switching is the unconscious shifting of attention from one activity to another. It also refers to the ability to switch the requirements of a task based on changing rules and requirements. For example, sorting is a common preschool activity that requires children to group objects based on a common feature, such as color, shape, or size. Task switching would occur when the teacher has a child sort objects based on color, re-sort them based on size, and sort them based on color again. For some children, switching focus to complete a task is simple. They are able to refocus their attention on the requirements and complete the activity successfully. For others, task switching can be a difficult challenge that confuses and frustrates them.

Flexible Thinking

Flexible thinking is a skill that helps people look at situations in different ways, find new solutions to solve problems, and shift gears when what is supposed to happen doesn't. Children who have no trouble adjusting to change are flexible thinkers. They easily adapt to different situations, such as adjustments to the school schedule or a sudden change in plans. Flexible thinking allows for adaptability throughout the school day.

Inflexible thinking is a maladaptive pattern that has a negative effect on children's success both academically and socially. Even with a predictable classroom schedule and routines, the school day constantly changes, and children encounter situations that require flexible thinking. Those who struggle with flexible thinking, as Kelsey does in the following example, are rigid in their thoughts and actions, which can have a negative impact on social interactions, play skills, and problem-solving abilities.

> Kelsey, a bright four-year-old, runs into her preschool classroom, excited to play in the kitchen area as she does every morning. When she gets to the pretend-play area, she discovers that the kitchen is missing. She looks around the classroom and sees her friends are busy doing other things. Some are building with blocks, while others merrily play dress-up. Kelsey stands in the middle of the room feeling frustrated that she cannot play the game she always does when she transitions from home to school. Her teacher explains to Kelsey that the toy kitchen broke and will not be back until tomorrow because it is being repaired. She suggests Kelsey play somewhere else, but Kelsey remains where she is, exclaiming, "I want to play with the kitchen like I always do!"

Kelsey is struggling with flexible thinking. She faces an unexpected change to her morning routine and, rather than shifting her attention as her friends did, remains fixed in her thinking.

When children like Kelsey struggle with attentional flexibility, they may seem rigid in their thoughts. They need the routine to stay the same, resist trying new games or activities, and may have difficulty with problem solving. Children who are not flexible thinkers may become overly frustrated when they transition from one activity to the next, when classmates don't follow the rules, or when friends suggest new ways to play a game.

Working Memory

Working memory, the second component of executive function, is a type of short-term memory that helps people hold onto important information long enough to use it. Different from long-term memory, working memory refers to the small amount of important information children need to retain to successfully engage in cognitive tasks and classroom activities. Working memory is like a mental to-do list, with the information stored only as long as it is useful. Once it is no longer needed, the to-do list disappears, freeing up space so that the child has the capacity to take in new and important information. For example, when you stop by the store to pick up a few things you need, you are using working memory to store those items and remember to purchase them. Once they've been purchased, there's no reason for you to remember the list, so you forget the information.

Working memory is responsible for:

- recalling and following instructions;
- carrying out instructions in the correct order;
- remembering where school items such as glue sticks, markers, and extra paper are located;
- recalling details during pretend-play activities;
- retelling a story; and
- socializing.

Children who have strong working-memory skills are better at recalling and following directions, organization, problem solving, and starting and finishing tasks and activities.

Children use this executive-function skill throughout the school day to learn and follow directions. Working memory helps them remember what they need to be paying attention to and then use that information to complete tasks and activities. When children struggle with working memory, they may be unable to keep track of what they are supposed to do. They may struggle to complete a task, abandoning it partway through because they have forgotten the rest of the steps required. Children with weak working-memory skills may:

- seem disorganized,
- have difficulty remembering what they want to say when called on to answer a question,

- struggle with problem solving,
- have trouble starting new or complex activities on their own,
- abandon activities before they are finished, and
- appear to be working hard but have little to show for it.

Working Memory Capacity

The *capacity*, or amount of working memory that can be stored at one time, increases as children grow and mature (Ahmed et al., 2022; Anderson et al., 2001). Young children are only able to hold a limited amount of information in their working memory at any given time. For example, toddlers may be able to remember and follow two-step directions, such as "First, put your shoes on. Then, we can go for a walk." But, they may not be able to follow more complex instructions, such as "First, put your toys away. Then, put your shoes on. Then, meet me at the door, and we will go for a walk." While a two-year-old may not be able to remember and follow all of these steps, a four-year-old should be able to pick up his toys, put on his shoes, and then meet his father at the door to go for a walk. It's important to recognize the limitations of children's working memory based on age and experience and to avoid requiring them to remember too many rules or difficult routines. Proper support will help them succeed at what they are capable of remembering.

When an activity is novel, each step needs to hold a place in a child's working memory. Children who have experience with an activity may remember some or all of the steps necessary to complete it, a skill known as *chunking*. Rather than needing to remember every step of the activity, children with prior knowledge can chunk together all or part of it. In the following example, some children have completed the class activity before, and many remember the steps required to complete their project successfully and in a timely manner. But for Roscoe, the activity is new to him. His working memory is more taxed than the students who have completed the activity in the past.

Ms. Rodgers has decided to introduce a new activity to her class: paper tearing. She knows this activity is good for improving fine-motor skills. She completed an example of a finished project the night before and is introducing it at circle time. "Today, we are going to make pictures that look like stained glass!" she says, holding up her project. "I made this by placing pieces of colored tissue paper on this sticky paper called contact paper." She points out the contact paper. "At your desks, you will find everything you need to make your own creation. First, you will choose the colors you want to use. Then, you will tear the tissue paper into small pieces. Then, you will remove the back of the contact paper to reveal the sticky side of it. And finally, you will stick the paper pieces on the contact paper in any design you choose." Ms. Rodgers begins to explain different design options when a child in her class states, "We did this last year in Ms. Langley's class! It was so fun." Most of the children nod their heads in agreement, remembering the activity from last year.

Ms. Rodgers dismisses the group, and everyone hurries to their desks. The children who were in Ms. Langley's class get to work right away, tearing paper and talking about the designs they are going to create. Roscoe, however, sits at his desk, unsure where to begin. This is Roscoe's first year going to school, and he struggles with most creative art projects. He watches his classmates busily tearing and sorting the tissue paper but doesn't join in. When Ms. Rodgers stops by his table, she asks him if he needs any help. "I don't know what to do," Roscoe replies. Timmy, a classmate at the same table, chimes in. "You're supposed to make this!" he says, holding up his almost complete project. "We made these a lot last year. They're so easy to make." Roscoe looks confused and asks Ms. Rodgers for help. She explains each step to Roscoe, demonstrating how to tear the paper and then how to sort the pieces by color. Finally, after hearing the directions again and seeing how to tear and sort the paper, Roscoe begins to work on his project.

Timmy and other children in the class have done this activity before. They are able to chunk together the steps required to complete a finished project because they have prior knowledge they can draw from. Roscoe, however, has never done a paper-tearing activity before. The activity is new to him, so he needs to hold a place in his working memory for every step required. He needs extra guidance and support from his classroom teacher to know how to begin the activity and the order of the steps required and needs a visual model to show him what the finished project could look like.

Inhibitory Control

Inhibitory control, the third component of executive function, is the ability to stop and think before reacting (Anderson, 2002). It allows children to repress an inappropriate thought or action and instead respond in a way that matches the task, activity, or social situation. Inhibitory control is also responsible for children's ability to focus on what is relevant, like the teacher's explanation or a group activity, while suppressing attention to everything else (Dowsett and Livesey, 2000). Children with strong inhibitory control can wait their turn, control their impulses, and persist at activities. They attend to what their teacher is saying or engage in a conversation with a friend while blocking out the unimportant visual and auditory events happening all around them.

Children who have strong inhibitory-control skills are better at:

- Waiting their turn
- Resisting temptation
- Suppressing irrelevant information
- Being persistent
- Controlling impulsive behaviors

Inhibitory control happens all the time at both a conscious and subconscious level. Successful inhibitory control requires continual monitoring of both the self and the immediate environment to suppress inappropriate responses. Many young children need help learning how to control their impulses. With practice and support, however, children can learn patience and self-control, as can be seen in the following example.

> Mila, an outgoing kindergartner, has worked hard throughout preschool to control her desire to answer every question, be the first in line, and win every game she plays in class. Many times, when she didn't get her way, Mila would cry and sulk, causing unwanted social interactions with her teachers and classmates. This year, she is applying the skills she's been taught, including taking a deep breath before she blurts out an answer or reminding herself when she plays a game with a friend, "It's only a game. It doesn't matter who wins or loses. What matters is having fun." With help from her preschool teachers, Mila's inhibitory control has matured over the past two years. On the first day of kindergarten, Mila sits quietly at circle time. She listens intently to her teacher and waits her turn to share with the class what she liked best about summer. When it's finally Mila's turn to share, she excitedly explains all the things she did over the summer. Next, Mila's teacher explains that some children will be assigned class jobs each week. Mila raises her hand quickly because she hopes she'll be chosen for one of the jobs, but she isn't. Mila is disappointed, but she hears her teacher say that the children who weren't chosen this week will most likely have a class job next week. She might have cried in prekindergarten, but Mila is now able to inhibit her reactions and remain calm.

Mila demonstrates inhibitory control as she waits her turn at circle time instead of blurting out a response. She also inhibits her emotional response as she refrains from crying or acting out when she isn't chosen for a classroom job.

In this example, we see that inhibitory control matures over time, with rapid development from ages two to five (Anderson, 2002). Preschool children will have less developed inhibitory control than children in kindergarten (Dowsett and Livesey, 2000). In a preschool classroom, it is still developmentally appropriate for some children to demonstrate big reactions when they don't get what they want, to struggle with delayed gratification and patience, and even to lash out at classmates. Over time, children's inhibitory control improves thanks to feedback and successful interactions.

Older children who continue to struggle with inhibitory control may act impulsively and ignore the classroom rules and established social norms to get what they want right when they want it. They may overreact when games and activities don't go their way, or they may throw tantrums. Their schoolwork may be rushed, and they may be easily distracted, focusing on everything going on around them instead of what they should be doing. Inhibitory control can be learned and, if a child struggles with it, can improve over time with practice and strategies.

There are two main types of inhibitory control:

- Attentional inhibition: the ability to block out irrelevant information such as visual and auditory distractions and focus on what matters
- Response inhibition: the ability to stop and think before acting

Attentional Inhibition

Attentional inhibition, or selective attention, is the brain's ability to focus on something important while tuning out other visual and auditory stimuli. Children must inhibit attending to visual and auditory distractions while listening to the teacher give instructions for a seated activity. They must learn how to attend to their classwork while surrounded by classmates who might be coughing or sneezing, fidgeting in their seats, or walking around. They must inhibit their attention to what is going on in the hallway or outside the window to maintain focus on the task at hand, such as lunch, play, or work. Furthermore, when children have a conversation with their peers, attentional control helps them focus on what the peer is saying instead of all the other conversations and noises in the classroom.

Response Inhibition

Response inhibition is the ability to pause before acting. Similar to self-control, response inhibition helps children think before they act to manage impulsive behaviors and respond appropriately to something. Children with strong inhibitory control are able to think about how their actions might affect themselves and the people around them before acting.

> Danny, a preschool child, really wants to see his classmate Levi's new Lego car that he's brought in for show and tell. Levi has been holding onto the car all morning, and Danny has asked repeatedly if he can see it. While Levi has shown it to him, he won't let Danny hold it. When another classmate—Levi's best friend, Ricky—asks to see it, Levi quickly hands it over to his friend. Danny immediately becomes upset but resists the urge to grab the toy from Ricky. He runs to his teacher and tells her what has happened, looking to her for support to manage his feelings.

In this situation, even though he becomes upset, Danny demonstrates strong response inhibition when he sees Levi hand over the Lego car to his best friend, Ricky. If Danny struggled with response inhibition, he might have grabbed the toy, pushed Levi, or thrown a tantrum.

Children who struggle with response inhibition in the classroom will have trouble inhibiting their responses and reactions. This may result in behaviors such as the following:

- Rushing their schoolwork
- Blurting out answers without waiting to be called on
- Disregarding the classroom rules and routines when they want something badly
- Writing or saying the first answer that comes to mind without thinking it through
- Throwing a tantrum when they do not get what they want right when they want it
- Struggling with patience and waiting their turn

Putting It All Together

When all three components of executive function work together, a child can translate a mental to-do list into a plan, execute the plan's steps in the correct order, and remember all the steps required while remaining attentive to the task and filtering out irrelevant information. As a result, the child is goal-driven and successful.

> Emmett is a kindergartener who loves astronauts and space and is really looking forward to meeting and listening to the guest speaker who will talk with the class about outer space. His working-memory skills help him remember the daily schedule and that the speaker is coming in after the class finishes circle time, centers, outdoor recess, and lunch. Since Emmett cannot tell time yet, this schedule is important for him to keep in mind. In combination with his inhibitory-control skills, he is able to refer to the posted schedule rather than pester his teacher about when the speaker will be coming into the classroom. Unfortunately, after lunch, Emmett's teacher tells the class that the speaker won't be able to come in until the next afternoon. Instead, she hands out a space-themed packet with coloring and other activities. Now, Emmett must use his inhibitory control and attentional flexibility skills to shift his focus to this new and unplanned activity.

Emmett illustrates strong executive-function skills. When working memory, attentional flexibility, and inhibitory control are practiced and talked about in the school setting, everyone benefits. Those with excellent executive-function skills—like Emmett—will lead by example, while those with emerging skills have the opportunity to learn these critical behaviors in a warm and nurturing environment. In the following chapter, we explore the connection between executive function and self-regulation, learning what self-regulation is and how to help support this skill in the classroom.

Chapter 2:

Self-Regulation and Executive Function

Throughout the school day, children rely on executive functioning to successfully engage in activities, socialize with peers, and stick with things even when they become difficult or boring. How well children are able to complete these activities is also largely dependent on their self-regulation skills. *Self-regulation* is the ability to remain calm and in control of oneself when faced with big emotions. Children who are able to regulate their emotions well are better able to draw upon their executive-function skills to stop, think, and then act, which, in turn, has a positive effect on social interactions, school success, learning, attention, and focus.

Combined with executive functioning, self-regulation helps children stay on task; focus on what is relevant; control their impulses and body movements no matter how excited, angry, or upset they become; and match behavior and social interactions to the situation. The better children are at self-regulation, the more capable they are at accessing executive-function skills to be successful throughout the school day.

Young children will demonstrate a wide range of self-regulation abilities. Preschool, kindergarten, and even first-grade children will most likely require support to develop and improve upon these skills. Some children may need help recognizing that something is upsetting or overly exciting. Others may have difficulty knowing how to calm down and take control of their emotions or behaviors on their own. Children with emerging or poorly developed self-regulation abilities may struggle in the classroom with sustained attention, impulse control, and remembering pertinent information.

Difficulties with Self-Regulation

Children with poor self-regulation may feel and react more intensely to something that bothers them than those who are able to remain calm. Children who frequently experience intense emotions that result in withdrawal, tantrums, or overly silly behaviors may be having difficulty with self-regulation. They are unable to cope with their feelings appropriately, which results in big emotional reactions. Additionally, some young children may not know how to manage the strong emotions they feel in response to new events, foods, games, and activities. They may act impulsively, destructively, or aggressively, as we see with Cooper in the following example.

> Ms. Franklin teaches prekindergarten at a Head Start program. She has created a warm and nurturing play-based classroom with a strong focus on supporting children's emotional regulation skills. One morning during center time, Ms. Franklin asks the children at the art center if they'd like to work on cutting skills. Each of the four children at the center agrees, so Ms. Franklin gets out paper, markers, and five pairs of scissors and places the materials in the middle of the table. It's close to Valentine's Day, so she shows them how to cut out a heart. First, Ms. Franklin folds a piece of paper in half the long way. Then, she draws an arching line from one corner of the folded paper up and around to the top, creating the pattern she will cut. Next, she shows the children the proper way to hold a pair of scissors before she begins to cut slowly and carefully along the line. Finally, when she's finished cutting, she unfolds the paper and reveals the heart shape she has created.
>
> One of the children, Jamal, decides he doesn't want to cut with scissors and, instead, chooses to draw and watch the others. Another child, Remi, states that she loves cutting with scissors. She

> grabs a pair of scissors and a sheet of paper and starts making little snips on the paper. The other two children in the group, Cooper and José, are very interested in copying Ms. Franklin and get to work. José talks with his classmates as he gathers up his materials. He folds his paper in half and copies the pattern Ms. Franklin made. Carefully, he cuts along the line from start to end and then shows off his finished product to the group. As José is finishing his heart, Cooper is just getting started. He seems a bit frustrated that José has already finished and begins to rush. Cooper remembers to fold the paper in half the long way, but, forgetting to draw a line, he starts to quickly cut out a shape. José watches him and exclaims, "You didn't make the line like Ms. Franklin did." Cooper looks at his work and then at Ms. Franklin's. He realizes José is right and immediately becomes upset. He throws the scissors across the table, rips up his paper, and yells at José to leave him alone.

When Cooper realized he had made a mistake, he became angry instead of grabbing a new piece of paper and starting over. He was unable to regulate his emotions and acted out aggressively toward José by yelling and throwing the scissors across the table. In this example, Cooper struggled with self-regulation, working memory, and inhibitory control.

Children who struggle with self-regulation exhibit challenging behaviors that are often disruptive. This may cause them to:

- quit difficult games and activities.
- sabotage activities when they feel frustrated or angry.
- become angry or upset quickly and struggle to calm down on their own.
- disrupt the class with overly silly or impulsive behavior.
- demand attention from caregivers to help them finish a game or activity.

Acting out, whether by avoidance, withdrawal, or being overly silly, is typically a sign of a maladaptive response to a thought or feeling. Children rarely act out for no reason. An important aspect of self-regulation is self-awareness. When children are self-aware, they can recognize how they are feeling and why. Before learning self-regulation skills, many children react to unfamiliar situations with a fight-or-flight response. This is especially true during times of stress or intense emotions. The response may prevent children from remaining calm and thinking before they act. Therefore, it is important to help children learn self-regulation skills in the classroom.

Using Self-Regulation to Support Executive Function

Children rely on executive function and self-regulation skills throughout the school day. They regulate their emotions so that they are able to think before they act, identify feelings, and inhibit inappropriate or unnecessary behaviors and actions. When children regulate themselves, they are better able to draw upon their executive functions. Strong self-regulation and executive-function skills allow children to:

- stop and ask for what they want rather than cry, lash out, or throw a tantrum.
- take turns with friends and patiently wait their turn while playing a game.
- pay attention during a story rather than act out or interact with children around them.
- wait in line without pushing or shoving.
- follow directions without demanding assistance from a peer or the classroom teacher.
- follow through to the end of an activity, even when it is hard or frustrating.

The following section describes how children's ability to self-regulate supports their executive-function skills of attentional flexibility, working memory, and inhibitory control.

Flexible Thinking and Self-Regulation

A change to the usual routine or activity may elicit strong feelings in some children. Children who are internally well regulated will be able to manage these feelings and shift their attention and focus without becoming upset. Children who are flexible thinkers can shift gears when what they thought was going to happen doesn't for some reason. They can also troubleshoot and solve problems in different ways. They adapt easily to changes and disruptions that occur throughout the school day.

Children must be flexible thinkers when they engage in imaginative play with their peers, when they play a familiar game in a new way, and when they engage in unstructured play on the playground. These times in the school day are typically child-led rather than teacher-driven, so children need strong self-regulation skills to successfully interact with their peers and engage in activities in the absence of an adult who can model self-regulation or co-regulate with children when needed. Children who struggle to regulate their emotions when they are faced with change may resist making the change or may become overly upset.

Task Switching and Self-Regulation

Task switching requires attention and focus as well as the flexibility to change from doing a task one way to doing it another way. The more well-regulated children are, the better they will be at remaining calm when they forget the rules or have to complete an activity differently from the way they previously did it. When children have a low tolerance for frustration and like when things remain the same, they may struggle to remain calm and in control of their emotions when faced with a change in a familiar activity. They may act out and refuse to engage with the activity.

> Ms. Thompson is an early childhood educator in a Montessori classroom. The children in her class range from three to five years of age. Sorting is a popular activity that she encourages the younger children to work on. All year long, the children have practiced sorting bears by color and are able to complete this

> work successfully, so Ms. Thompson has decided to change the activity to make it more challenging. She removes the bears from the sorting station and replaces them with colorful rocks that vary in size and shape. Children can now sort not only by color but also by shape and size.
>
> Kyan, a three-year-old, loves the sorting station. He enjoys the repetitive work and is visibly satisfied when he completes his work successfully. Kyan is also a child who tends to become frustrated easily. He seeks out the teacher more than the other children do, requesting help whenever he thinks he may not do something correctly. When it is time for independent work, Kyan chooses sorting as his activity. He quickly sorts the rocks by color and calls Ms. Thompson over to see what he's done. Ms. Thompson praises his effort and remarks upon his success. Then, she asks him to sort the rocks again but by size instead of color. Kyan looks confused, so Ms. Thompson demonstrates for him, pointing out that there are small rocks, medium-sized rocks, and big rocks. When she's sorted a few into the new categories, she encourages Kyan to try. He picks up a small white rock and places it with a group of large rocks that are mostly white and gray. Ms. Thompson points out the error and shows him that the small rock belongs with the other small rocks. She reminds him that he is now sorting by size rather than color and encourages him to try again. "No!" Kyan yells. "That's not how you do it. I want to sort the bears!" Ms. Thompson explains that the bears aren't a part of the sorting station anymore and again encourages Kyan to try to sort with the rocks. He refuses and pushes the materials away from him, causing the rocks to scatter across the table and floor. When Ms. Thompson asks him to pick up the rocks, he shouts no again and runs away from the table.

Kyan resorted to sorting by color—as he'd done all year—when he placed the small white rock with the larger rocks. When Ms. Thompson reminded him that the task had changed and they were sorting the rocks by size, Kyan was unable to regulate his emotions and abandoned the activity. The next time Kyan attempts the sorting station, Ms. Thompson must support both Kyan's regulation skills and his attentional flexibility if he is going to successfully sort the rocks based on their size.

Children's self-regulation skills have a substantial impact on attentional flexibility. The better children are at controlling their emotions when faced with a change in routine or a switch in the rules to complete an activity, the easier it will be to achieve success. When children can't manage their emotions in their own way, they will struggle with attentional flexibility.

Filtering and Self-Regulation

The school day is filled with sights and sounds, side conversations, and other distractions that children need to learn to ignore while simultaneously paying attention to and remembering relevant information. Children who are internally well regulated are able to remain calm and in control of their thoughts and feelings. This self-control allows them to focus on what they need to and remember what they should. Children who struggle with self-regulation may become overwhelmed in noisy or visually distracting environments because they find it difficult to filter out distracting information. This difficulty causes some children to disengage in the activity that they should be attending to.

Working Memory and Self-Regulation

During the early learning years, children are not only learning social, preliteracy, math, and fine- and gross-motor skills, they are also learning how to remember, what to remember, and what they need to focus on and attend to. When learning new activities, they need to both *remember* and *use* the information stored in their working memory. Similarly, they need to recall classroom rules, routines, and social norms. Strong self-regulation skills ensure that children are calm and able to attend to their teachers, their classmates, and what is going on around them to take in important information, filter out what isn't important, and then access that information in their working memory to complete tasks and activities successfully.

These working-memory skills develop over time with practice and maturation. However, the more regulated children are in the classroom, the more capable they are of learning both *how* and *what* to remember.

When children are unable to regulate their emotions well, they will not be able to reach the calm and organized state of mind necessary to remember and follow rules and instructions.

Some young children have exceptional working-memory capacity and can store and access large amounts of information in their working memory. Other children may have a lower capacity and are only able to retain small amounts of information in their working memory. Strong self-regulation skills support working-memory capacity in the classroom because well-regulated children will have more capacity to draw upon the established rules and expectations in classroom activities and social situations.

When children feel intensely and then react intensely, they can struggle to participate successfully in the established routines and classroom activities. Those who struggle with self-regulation must manage a lot to be successful in the classroom. Intense emotions such as excitement, anger, fear, and frustration diminish working-memory capacity because children focus on their emotions instead of listening to and retaining the information they need to remember.

Inhibitory Control and Self-Regulation

Self-regulation supports inhibitory control and allows children to manage their impulses without overreacting when they are not able to get what they want when they want it. Remaining patient is challenging for many young children, especially when they really want to win a game, blurt out an answer, or be first in line. Self-regulation and inhibitory control encourage patience, strong social skills, and a calm state of mind. Recall Mila from chapter 1, the kindergartner working to inhibit her impulse to blurt out answers and be first at everything. While she was in preschool, Mila could not regulate her emotions well when she didn't get her way. She'd cry and sulk if she wasn't called on to answer a question or lead the class during transitions. In kindergarten, her inhibitory-control skills and self-regulation skills have matured.

With the support she received from her preschool teachers, Mila developed the ability to regulate her emotions when faced with a situation that required her to inhibit her blurting or her desire to be first. Now, she remains patient and uses self-calming strategies to remain in control of her emotions.

In the next section of this chapter, we explore strategies to nurture and support the development of self-regulation skills through co-regulation, an interactive strategy that teaches young children self-regulation skills through modeling, mirroring, and teaching and talking about feelings.

Using Co-Regulation to Support Self-Regulation

Co-regulation is an excellent tool to help teach children how to manage emotions in a regulated and functional way. Most young children learn how to navigate the world around them by imitating the emotions and reactions they see in familiar adults and caregivers. During the early learning years, self-regulation develops in part due to the interactions children have with their caregivers, including their teachers while they are at school (Montroy et al., 2016). Co-regulation happens when caregivers and familiar adults help children calm down when they become upset by understanding and processing the many emotions they are experiencing in the moment (Murray, Rosanbalm, Christopoulos, and Hamoudi, 2014). This is especially important in preschool and even prekindergarten classrooms because young children haven't had time to develop strong self-regulation skills. Effective co-regulation strategies include:

- modeling a calm self,
- teaching and talking about feelings, and
- mirroring calming strategies.

Modeling a Calm Self

Young children need many opportunities to learn and practice self-regulation. The more they do, the more likely they are to acquire strong regulation skills they can rely on throughout their lives. Adults who are calm and in control of their emotions demonstrate how to regulate their emotions to the children around them. When caregivers consistently respond in big, angry, or overreactive ways, children may mimic these actions and fail to develop successful self-regulation. Guiding children to respond calmly to big feelings or stimuli will help combat dysregulation and challenging behaviors and will lay a foundation for improved self-regulation the next time they encounter these stressors. In contrast, punishment, scolding, and impatience may cause children to believe that their big reactions are justified. This will likely lead to prolonged behavioral issues and classroom-management problems. When teachers and caregivers act calm and in control, they set an example for children and confirm that this is the proper behavior.

Teaching and Talking about Feelings

Providing a nurturing and consistent school environment rich in sensory play and activities helps develop self-regulation skills in all children. In a classroom environment where self-regulation is seen as a skill that needs to be discussed and developed, children can learn appropriate and adaptive responses to difficult feelings or social situations. Each time they experience strong emotions, children will have new tools to maintain a calm demeanor and remain in control of their reactions.

Talking to and teaching children about emotions will diminish challenging behaviors over time. The purpose of identifying feelings is to develop self-awareness and the ability to understand what another person is experiencing. Once a teacher sees that children can identify their feelings, she should encourage the children to practice pausing and reflecting on their emotions. This introspection helps them understand why they are feeling a certain way. Then, when children understand what emotions are and how different types of interactions elicit different emotions, they are ready to learn and practice adaptive responses. Teaching children about feelings and emotions helps them regulate their emotions in a wide variety of situations. They learn that it is okay to *feel* strongly about something, but instead of *reacting* strongly, they learn to reflect on the following:

- What am I feeling right now?
- What made me feel this way?
- What do I *want* to do?
- Is it appropriate?
- What have I learned how to do instead?

Mirroring Calming Strategies

Showing children how to use calming strategies is another way to cultivate their self-regulation skills. When co-regulating with a child who is upset, rather than meeting them at their heightened emotional state, talk quietly and slowly. Breathe deeply, and encourage the child to do the same. Encourage the child to copy your actions, matching their breath and body to mirror yours. Then, once they've calmed down a bit, talk with them about strategies they can use to regain control of their emotions by following the above sequence of steps.

Putting It All Together

The stronger their executive-function and self-regulation skills, the better young children are at sustaining their focus and succeeding in their play, learning, and social activities. Well-regulated children are more able to access their executive-function skills when they need them, which ensures they are they are better at flexible thinking, problem solving, and troubleshooting and have stronger social connections with their peers. Supporting self-regulation throughout the school day helps children control their emotional reactions and remain calm and attentive to what matters. Embedding sensory strategies throughout the day also supports executive function. In the next chapter, we learn what sensory strategies are and how to implement them in the classroom to support all children's attentional flexibility, working memory, and inhibitory control.

Chapter 3:

Sensory Strategies to Improve Executive-Function Skills

Sensory strategies are activities that engage the senses to help children become and stay focused, which is an important part of executive function. All children can benefit from sensory strategies at some point during the school day because they support strong executive-function skills. In addition to helping with focus and attention span, employing sensory strategies throughout the school day can make learning more interactive, engaging, and exciting for children. This chapter describes what the senses are, what an arousal level is, and how an alert and calm level of arousal supports strong executive-function skills. You will also learn specific sensory strategies and activities that teachers can embed into the classroom to help children focus, pay attention, remember what they need to, maintain self-control, and think flexibly throughout the day.

Understanding the Senses and Arousal Levels

The senses include those that most people are familiar with: touch, sight, hearing, taste, and smell. But, there are two additional senses: the vestibular sense and proprioception. The *vestibular sense* is responsible for balance and how a person's body interprets and responds to movement (Ayres, 1972). Movement input triggers the vestibular sense and can have an alerting and calming effect on people. In the classroom, this type of input has a positive effect on attention and focus (Ayres, 1972). *Proprioception* is the way the body senses movement and understands how to move through space. It is responsible for motor-planning movements, such as picking up a glass of water, drinking from it, and putting it back down again without spilling anything, and for being able to walk through the classroom without bumping into things. Sensory activities that involve the proprioception system are those that create tension within the body, such as pushing, pulling, and carrying heavy objects. The main purpose of using movement and proprioception sensory strategies in the classroom is to help children attain and maintain an optimal level of arousal so they can focus on what they need to, when they need to, for as long as they need to (Ayres, 1972).

Arousal level refers to how awake and alert a person is. When people are sleeping, their arousal level is very low. When they are highly agitated or stressed, their arousal level is very high. An optimal level of arousal allows children to perform to the best of their ability, remain flexible when things need to change, and control their impulses. They are both alert and calm, allowing them to focus and learn. Some children will benefit from sensory strategies that decrease their arousal level, while others will benefit from inputs that make them more alert and engaged. When children's arousal levels match the demands of the task or activity, children are able to focus and access their executive-function skills.

Arousal level fluctuates throughout the day, which makes it important for children's energy levels to match the activity they are participating in. For example, during rest/nap time, a low arousal level is desirable for falling asleep. On the playground, however, children's arousal levels may rise so they can enjoy movement games and playground equipment. In the classroom, an optimal level of arousal allows children to focus and learn. When children are not able to focus on what they are learning, it is difficult for them to access their executive-function skills. When they are focused, they can better access their executive-function skills to be successful with what they are learning.

To fully support strong executive-function skills, it is not enough for children to reach the level of arousal in which they are both alert and calm. They also need to maintain this level so they can participate in classroom routines, follow rules, learn, and socialize for the duration of the school day. Educators can implement additional sensory strategies that engage the tactile, vestibular, and proprioception senses to help children sustain an optimal level of arousal during the difficult parts of their school day. For example, some children struggle to pay attention during large-group learning such as circle time. Because the child-to-teacher ratio is high, learning in a large group requires more self-control, which is hard for many young children. These children may have difficulty engaging the executive-function skills necessary to pay attention to the person talking, remember what they are supposed to, or sit still and not distract children around them. Sitting on a movement cushion during circle time might provide children with the movement they are craving while supporting their ability to focus, allowing them to access their executive-function skills. For other children, adding a tactile component such as a fidget toy during circle time or manipulatives during math assignments might help them remain attentive and focused on their classwork. In the following section, you will learn specific movement strategies to help support children's executive functions in the classroom.

Movement Input to Support Arousal Level and Executive Function

Sensory strategies that involve movement, balance, and coordination support executive-function skills because they help children remain alert and calm throughout the school day (Michel and Bimmüller, 2023; van der Veer, Cantell, Minnaert, and Houwen, 2022). When the day offers children regular opportunities to exercise and move their bodies, they will be more able to learn and retain information. All children benefit from movement input because it helps them attain and maintain an optimal level of arousal. For children who struggle to sit still and pay attention, providing regular opportunities to engage in balance and coordination activities will help them focus on what they need to, remember what they are supposed to, and have better self-control.

Experts believe that young children's attention span is approximately two to three times their age (Diamond, 2002). This means that a three-year-old's attention span is about six to nine minutes, a four-year-old's attention span is about eight to twelve minutes, and a five-year-old's attention span is about ten to fifteen minutes. Some young children struggle to remain seated and attentive to an activity for an age-appropriate amount of time. This means that they are unable to sustain their focus on one activity for as long as their same-age peers. After a short time, they may become distracted, zone out, or crave movement input. When they crave movement, they may intentionally fall out of their chairs, refuse to stay seated, or fidget in their seats. If they are working hard just to sit still, they have little attentional capacity left to focus on their schoolwork.

When children engage in regular sensory play that involves movement, many are able to store up that input and access it later during seated activities. Providing opportunities to move, work on balance, or hold yoga poses between sedentary times in the day will help them sit for longer periods and concentrate on the tasks on hand. To support seated attention and focus, consider providing opportunities for movement in two- to ten-minute intervals each hour throughout the day—but especially before circle time, mealtimes, and seated work. For example, encourage children to complete obstacle courses, dance, and play Freeze Tag. Activities like these will help them sit and focus during circle time, at centers, and at mealtimes.

Balance and coordination activities not only provide children with movement input, but they also help children improve their core muscles, which will support sustained attention during seated activities. Sitting on the floor during circle time, in a chair upright during mealtime, and at a desk to focus on work requires a great deal of balance and core strength. Children who struggle with balance or have weak core muscles may seek movement to help keep themselves upright and engaged. When they do so, they have limited capacity for working memory. Engaging in activities that improve balance will help children sit for longer periods without becoming fatigued. Encouraging them to engage in these types of activities during transitions into and out of the classroom provides natural opportunities for this input without adding tasks to the school day.

Offer balance and coordination activities like these during transitions:

- Walking along a masking-tape "balance beam"
- Playing Hopscotch
- Playing standing-in-place games such as standing on one foot and then the other, then doing this with their eyes closed

Children can walk along a masking-tape line or play Hopscotch while transitioning out of the classroom, down the hallway, or to the playground. These activities allow children to engage in extra movement input as they shift from one part of the day to the next. Games in which preschool-aged children stand in place and challenge their balance could occur while they are waiting in the hallway during bathroom breaks or waiting to come back inside after playing on the playground.

Embedding sensory strategies within the school day allows children to access these tools when they need support. For example, many young children struggle with attention and focus at the end of the school day. They have spent the morning and early afternoon responding in a flexible way when changes and disruptions occur, remembering what they need to, and maintaining self-control. In the final moments of the day, embedding activities such as music and movement during circle time or hands-on learning with manipulatives during centers will support flexible thinking, working memory, and inhibitory control.

Movement is not the only type of sensory strategy that supports children's attention, focus, and executive function in the classroom. In the next section, we explore engaging in sensory-play activities; being mindful of lighting, furniture placement, and classroom design; and reducing unnecessary visual and auditory distractions to support executive-function skills.

Sensory Play to Support Executive-Function Skills

Play is one of the primary ways that young children develop their executive-function skills. When children play, they can master skills without the threat of failure. They learn how to take turns, how to share limited resources, how to communicate, and what to do when they encounter something they don't like. This requires flexible thinking, task switching, working memory, and self-control.

Sensory play involves activities that engage children's senses, including their sense of balance and movement. Adding sensory components to an activity enhances children's learning exponentially. Studies show that sensory play helps children calm down when they feel anxious, overwhelmed, or angry. It also helps them develop mindfulness, improve impulse control, decrease behavioral outbursts, and improve flexible thinking skills (Chen, Yang, Chi, and Chen, 2013; Losinski, Sanders, and Wiseman, 2016). Through sensory play, children develop executive-function skills that they can use during other parts of the school day.

Supporting Attentional Flexibility through Sensory Play

One of the best strategies to support attentional flexibility, and flexible thinking skills in particular, is to encourage children to engage in open-ended sensory play. A common open-ended sensory activity is the sensory bin—a box, baking tray, bowl, or other container that is filled with messy materials, such as sand, water, slime, or shaving cream, as well as items to manipulate. This type of activity encourages imaginative play and exploration and leads to flexible thinking, problem solving, working-memory skills, and self-control. Children tend to enjoy open-ended sensory play because there is no set way to engage in the activity. They also learn important executive-function skills while enjoying the free-play activities.

How to Make a Sensory Bin

1. Start with a container. Note that children may engage differently in sensory play based on the size and type of container. A large container can accommodate multiple children at one time and will encourage cooperative play; a small container, such as a baking sheet or bowl, allows for individual and parallel play. Consider containers such as the following:

   - A sensory table for large classrooms
   - A large plastic bin with a lid for small-group play
   - Baking sheets, bowls, or muffin tins for individual sensory play

2. Add the base material. The base material can be dry (packaging peanuts, shredded paper, yarn, pompoms, sand, kinetic sand) or wet (water, water beads, shaving cream, slime, playdough). A wet base is messy and may stick to the child's clothing or skin as well as any items you add to the bin. A dry base is messy but will not stick to clothing, skin, or the items you add to the bin.

3. Choose the add-ins. Add-ins can include objects that match the theme of a lesson or the current season. For example, these could be letters, numbers, colors, or shapes to help with cognitive and preliteracy skills. They might be toy vehicles or animals that support a learning module about transportation, the jungle, or reptiles. Switch out the add-ins on a regular basis to support what children are learning and keep them interested.

Supporting Working Memory through Sensory Play

Cooperative sensory play supports children in developing patience, turn-taking, and the ability to listen to and follow rules. This type of sensory play can also help them develop working-memory skills. Some young children struggle with working memory, which hinders their ability to successfully complete tasks and engage in activities. Participating in sensory play is highly engaging and may motivate children to achieve success with the activity. Also, adding parameters and loose directions requires children to use their working memory to remember how to complete the sensory activity.

Ideas for sensory play that supports working memory include the following:

- Create a giant cardboard-box collage with empty boxes, masking tape, and paint.
- Fingerpaint with pudding or shaving cream at an easel or at a table with a small group.
- Create a homemade marble run with cardboard tubes, tape, and marbles.

Each of these activities is highly engaging and has steps to follow to create a final product, but there is no one right way for the finished product to turn out. This shifts the emphasis of the activity from the final product to the process, supporting the development of working-memory skills and task completion.

Supporting Inhibitory Control through Sensory Play

Through open-ended sensory play, children can also develop social skills, impulse control, and patience. Because there is no wrong way to engage in an open-ended sensory play activity, children don't need a specific item to be successful. When resources are limited—for example, if there are only two spoons or one spoon strainer at the sensory table—they may want to engage with the item but realize that they don't need to. This combination helps children learn inhibitory-control skills, including the following:

- Waiting their turn
- Sharing limited resources
- Asking for something instead of just taking it

For example, when children play at a sand and water table, they spend time scooping, pouring, and dumping alongside their classmates. When there are fewer things to scoop, pour, and mix than there are children, children learn how to wait their turn, ask for a toy, and play cooperatively with others. During open-ended sensory play, children learn inhibitory-control skills that they can access during more challenging parts of the school day.

Importance of the Classroom Environment

The classroom environment plays an important role in supporting children's ability to use their executive-function skills. A classroom that has minimal distractions, clear rules, and predictable routines will support flexible thinking, smooth transitions, self-control, and working-memory skills. Calm, nurturing environments designed to support executive functions allow children to learn about and practice executive-function skills.

First, consider the physical environment itself. It's not possible to change the size and shape of the room or the natural lighting options. But, with careful consideration, you can make the most of the space and lighting by placing furniture consistently; creating open space so children can move around the classroom safely without bumping into others; offering visual and auditory supports to help children remember classroom rules and routines; reducing visual and auditory distractions; and keeping natural light sources free from obstruction.

Reduce Visual and Auditory Distractions

A classroom that is noisy and full of visual distractions makes it difficult for many children to filter out those stimuli. Children who struggle with filtering will find it difficult to concentrate on what they should, like a conversation with a friend, directions from the teacher, or the task at hand because their attention is divided between these important things and the distractions. Reducing visual and auditory distractions will make it easier for children to focus on the activity or person they need to at that moment. Common visual distractions include the following:

- Clutter
- Disorganized classroom materials
- Walls that are full of visual aids, student work, and so on, with little blank space
- Overly colorful classroom

Common auditory distractions include the following:

- Objects that make inconsistent noise, such as a fan or heater
- Analog clocks that tick
- Overhead lights that hum
- Open windows
- Doors to the hallway
- Chatty classmates

Lighting and Furniture Placement

Proper lighting not only affects children's ability to see what they are working with, but it also influences their energy levels, focus, and attention. When possible, replace overhead fluorescent lights with LED bulbs; LED lighting is considered the best artificial light. Fluorescent bulbs have been found to emit a harsh light that causes fatigue, loss of focus, and eye strain in many people (Smolders and de Kort, 2013). Maximize natural light sources as much as possible, and consider placing learning centers in a space where there is a lot of natural light.

Next, think about the placement of tables for learning centers and mealtimes. The design and placement of the tables will affect how children socialize with one another, noise levels, and distractions. For example, in a class of fifteen preschool children, three semicircular tables allow five children and one adult to sit comfortably at each table. Each child will have enough room to manage their personal space and sit close enough to their peers to benefit from social interactions. They'll also be within easy earshot of the teacher or aide sitting at the table and will be heard if they have a question or ask for help. These tables can be used later in the school day for three separate learning stations, easily dividing up both the activities and the children.

Furniture arrangement provides the primary structure of the classroom. This structure gives children a sense of security and confidence as they independently navigate the room and the materials within it. Consider the number of children in the classroom, the size of the classroom, and the permanent fixtures, such as doors, windows, closets, and sinks.

Think about which sensory spaces are important for the children in the class. These might include a movement space, a cozy corner, or a calm-down space. They should be placed in a part of the classroom that is separated from the circle-time area and learning centers, easy to access, and safe for play and exploration. Arrange furniture to define different parts of the room, such as the following:

- Cozy corner
- Library area
- Pretend-play area
- Sensory and art area
- Music and movement area
- Seated learning areas
- Circle-time area

Storage Solutions

In an organized classroom, children are more organized and better able to focus on activities. Storing materials in closed containers that are out of view when not in use—and also located in a consistent spot—cuts down on clutter, organizes children's work and play spaces, and allows them to find what they need to be successful in activities. Consistently storing items that are not in use also cuts down on distractibility. When children can't see items that aren't relevant to the task or activity at hand, they are less likely to become distracted by them.

Designated Sensory Spaces for Every Classroom

Designating specific parts of the classroom as sensory spaces provides children with safe, inviting experiences where they can move, calm down, and explore. They can use these spaces during centers, at morning drop-off, right before pickup, or when they feel frustrated or overwhelmed. The most common sensory areas include a calm-down area, a movement space, and a tactile area.

Each sensory space should be thoughtfully designed and introduced to children so they know when and how to use it. Teach children how to use these spaces by allowing them to explore the area and the objects within it. Model how they might use the space when they need to calm down, get their wiggles out, or just have a quiet moment to themselves. Visiting sensory spaces when children are calm and attentive allows them to learn what they can do to calm down or regain focus when they are struggling to do so. Modeling thoughts, feelings, and actions for children will help them know when they might benefit from visiting a sensory space and what they might do once in the space.

Calm-Down Area

> At the start of the school year, Ms. Phillips designed a cozy corner in her kindergarten classroom. During the first few weeks of school, she brought her students into the space and allowed them to explore the objects in the cozy corner. Then, she modeled how to use the objects as a way to calm down. During circle time and small-group learning, Ms. Phillips talked with the children about how to identify and understand feelings. They read books containing characters with strong feelings. They explored feeling charts, and they worked on labeling feelings as they felt them through the day.

> One morning, Ms. Phillips accidentally knocked over her cup of coffee, spilling it all over herself and her desk. Recognizing this as an opportunity to tie strong feelings to using the cozy corner, Ms. Phillips gathered the class's attention and described her thoughts and feelings. "Right now, I feel mad that I spilled my coffee. I really wanted to drink it. And I'm mad because I spilled coffee on my pants and now they are wet and dirty. I feel mad in my body, so I think I am going to visit the cozy corner so I can practice calming down." She sat down in the cozy corner, modeled some deep breathing, and interacted with some of the objects in the space. After a few minutes, she addressed the class, "I feel better now. I know it was just an accident, and accidents happen. Plus, in a little while, I can go to the staff lounge and make myself another coffee."

Ms. Phillips modeled for her students how to identify feelings, how to use the cozy corner to calm down, and, once calm, how to problem solve and find a solution to move on with her day.

A serene sensory space is a part of the classroom where children may go to calm down when they become upset or overwhelmed. This space can be called the quiet corner, the cozy corner, the calm-down area, or something similar. Encourage the children to use this space when they feel a big emotion and need a few moments to calm down.

When creating a calming space, start with comfortable seating options where children can relax, such as beanbag chairs, oversized pillows, floor cushions, or gym mats. Add items that children may access for calming sensory inputs, including:

- Visual soothers
  - Sand timers
  - I Spy tubes
  - Kaleidoscopes
  - Look-and-feel books

- Tactile inputs
    - Fidget toys (that should remain in the sensory space)
    - Stuffed animals or toys that vibrate
    - Fabrics to interact with, such as scarves, silk, and faux fur
    - Fluffy pillows

Teach the children how to use this space so that they know how to transition to the space without disrupting the rest of the class. Show them how to correctly interact with the items in the space, and remind them to use the space when they need to rather than just when they want to.

Movement Space

The purpose of a movement space is to allow children to safely receive movement input during the school day. Designating a movement space offers children the opportunity to engage in activities that provide vestibular and/or proprioception input without leaving the classroom. Create a specific place in the classroom where children can access movement inputs by, for example, rocking in a rocking chair; shaking, clapping, tapping, and dancing with musical instruments; or doing yoga, jumping, or dancing on a gym mat. Also, consider adding an exercise ball placed in a plastic laundry basket, which allows children to bounce on the ball while it remains in one place.

Tactile Space

A tactile space is an important part of an early learning classroom because it provides children with sensory-rich opportunities to work on developing motor skills, social skills, problem-solving, inhibitory control, and attentional flexibility. Provide options for open-ended sensory play, such as sensory bins, tables, or troughs; a painting station; and a sand and water table.

In this space, children learn how to be flexible thinkers because there is no set way to play or succeed with the activity. They learn task-switching skills as they scoop, pour, dump, shake, and manipulate paintbrushes while playing in a cooperative, open-ended way. They work on problem-solving skills as they explore sensory bins or sand and water tables. They engage with peers and learn important inhibitory-control skills, such as waiting their turn, sharing limited resources, cleaning up messes, and navigating conflict. Once they learn these skills while engaging in open-ended play, they can use them during other parts of the school day.

Embedding Sensory Strategies in Daily Activities

Educators can embed sensory activities into the classroom to target the three components of executive function: attentional flexibility, working memory, and inhibitory control.

Supporting Attentional Flexibility

Support children's attentional flexibility by incorporating extra sensory inputs such as the following throughout the day:

- Offer fidgets during circle time
- Let children access manipulatives while learning
- Let children get movement input by sitting on a cushion or exercise ball

These strategies will help children be better able to switch their focus from one person, task, or activity to another in response to a changing situation.

Supporting Working Memory

Educators can support working memory through visual, movement, and proprioception sensory strategies. Sensory activities that require both a strong visual focus and memory skills, such as I Spy, treasure hunts, and look-and-find books, can help children focus and sustain their attention. They also offer opportunities for practicing working-memory skills. These types of visual sensory activities are both open-ended and structured, a combination that provides a highly stimulating visual experience and requires working-memory skills. There is no particular order or need to find all of the hidden objects, so children can work on developing working-memory skills through an activity that promotes success. When they feel like they are successful at an activity, children may be motivated to stick with the activity longer, giving them more opportunities to work on their working-memory skills.

How to Make an I Spy Bottle or Bag

An I Spy bottle is easy to make and encourages visual focus, sustained attention, and the ability to stay seated and engaged in one activity for an age-appropriate amount of time. Rather than just asking children to find objects in a book or on a piece of paper, I Spy bottles require them to shake, turn, and interact with the bottle. This added sensory requirement increases attention and focus.

1. Start with the container. Use a plastic water bottle or any clear plastic container that has a sealable lid. You could also use a heavy-duty, one-gallon freezer bag (double-bagged).
2. Fill the container or bag two-thirds full with a dry base that will move easily in the container. Options include colored sand, shredded paper, cotton balls, and pompoms.
3. Choose the add-ins. They may be themed, such as animals, letters, or numbers, or they may simply be items that are interesting to look at. Do not overfill the container; add just enough materials to let everything move freely.
4. Seal the bottle with superglue, hot glue, or duct tape. Seal the I Spy bag with duct tape.
5. On a piece of card stock or an index card, create a visual key with the add-in items so children know what they are looking for. A photograph that shows each of the add-ins works well as a visual key for preliterate children. Laminate the key for durability. Children may use dry-erase markers to check off the items on the key as they are found.

Sensory strategies with a movement focus excite and motivate young children as well as improve their focus and attention. Movement activities that have rules or ordered steps support working-memory skills. Examples of this type of movement sensory strategy include obstacle courses and treasure hunts. For both activities, children must move around the classroom (or outdoors) and follow directions to be successful.

Classroom Obstacle Course

Creating an obstacle course in the classroom is a fun, easy, and inexpensive way to provide children with movement opportunities that encourage working-memory skills. To complete an obstacle course successfully, children must remember the order and sequence of the course. By crawling, jumping, and walking through the course, they receive movement input while practicing working memory. Teachers could include this type of movement activity before seated activities each day. Switching the order of the steps or changing out steps in the obstacle course will ensure that children remain engaged in the activity and use their working-memory skills to be successful.

1. Set up the obstacle course in an open area where there is enough space for children to move safely.
2. At the start of the obstacle course, place a straight, curved, or zigzag line of masking tape on the floor for children to walk along.
3. At the end of the tape line, place a cushion on the floor for children to jump over.
4. A few feet away from the pillow, place a chair for children to walk around or crawl under.
5. Create a finish line with masking tape so children know they've completed the course.

Demonstrate and describe the steps to the course so the children will know what to do and in what order.

Classroom Treasure Hunt

Engaging in a treasure hunt around the classroom or on the playground is a fun way for children to move their bodies while working on following directions and using working-memory skills. Set up the treasure hunt by hiding clues and the treasure. Clues may be simple drawings or photos of items within the classroom that children have to find in sequential order. The final clue will lead to the hidden treasure, which may be a sweet treat or a note congratulating the children.

In pairs, small groups, or on their own, invite the children to begin the treasure hunt with the first clue, which leads them to the next clue. This continues until each clue and the treasure have been found.

Set a time limit by starting a visual timer and giving the class reminders as the time gets close to the end. Assist children as needed, but encourage and praise problem-solving, following directions, and remembering skills throughout the activity.

Proprioception inputs that are rhythmic in nature may help with memory and attention when included in an activity where working memory needs support. Rhythmic proprioception inputs include:

- bouncing on a therapy ball,
- tapping the floor or legs while seated,
- snapping fingers,
- clapping, and
- jumping up and down in place.

Pairing rhythmic proprioception input with singing or saying a sequence of events or directions to complete a task will support children's working memory.

> Pilar struggles to remember the morning routine on her own. Although she has been in kindergarten for a few weeks, she still tends to forget the steps she should follow when she gets

to school. This is her first experience at school, so following rules and routines in a group is new. Most of the other children have attended preschool or daycare and have no difficulty placing their things in their cubbies, washing their hands, signing in, and then finding a book to look at or a quiet activity to engage in before the school day begins. Each morning, Pilar seems confused and disorganized when she enters the classroom. Sometimes, she remembers to place her things in her cubby; other times, she drops them on the floor and begins to play. Ms. Ilana, the classroom teacher, has reminded Pilar of the morning routine to transition into the classroom, but Pilar seems to forget what she needs to do each day.

One morning, Ms. Ilana greets Pilar at the door to walk her through the morning routine. Instead of just stating the order of activities Pilar must complete, Ms. Ilana sings and claps out the steps. She sings the following to the tune of "Frère Jacques":

First your cubby. First your cubby.
Then wash hands. Then wash hands.
Now it's time to sign in. Now it's time to sign in.
Then find a book. Then find a book.

Ms. Ilana claps to the beat of the song and sings it repeatedly until Pilar has completed each of the steps. She also encourages Pilar to clap to the song. After a week of singing and clapping out the steps of the morning routine, Pilar can remember the steps and complete them in the correct order.

Supporting Inhibitory Control

Inhibitory control allows children to repress an inappropriate thought or action and respond in a way that matches the task, activity, or social situation. This skill is also responsible for sustaining focus on what matters and filtering out irrelevant things, such as people passing in the hallway or children talking. Children must continually monitor both themselves and their immediate environment to suppress inappropriate responses, such as stealing a toy, blurting out an answer, or leaving a learning activity to play with a desired toy. Providing children with sensory strategies that help them focus on what they should and filter out irrelevant stimuli will help support strong inhibitory-control skills throughout the school day.

Classrooms that are designed to be quiet, consistent, and free of unnecessary visual and auditory distractions support inhibitory control because children are better able to focus on what they should instead of what they want to. Young children are still learning about what is relevant and irrelevant, so classrooms that are noisy and visually distracting may lead to difficulties with inhibitory control. When toys and other objects are left out around the classroom, children who struggle with self-control may find it difficult to inhibit their strong desire to grab and play with a toy instead of engaging with what the rest of the class is doing.

> Alonzo loves to play with a train set during free-choice time. When free time ends, he often finds it hard to clean up the train area and transition to a different learning activity. When reassured by his teacher that the trains will be available to play with later, he is able to clean up and move on. His teacher makes sure to store the train set and all highly desired free-choice toys in solid-colored bins so children are not visually distracted by them when they are supposed to focus on other learning activities. When children such as Alonzo see toys or activities they really like, it can be hard for them to maintain self-control and avoid playing with them.

Strategies to reduce distracting visual and auditory inputs in the classroom include:

- keeping the classroom furniture in the same place,
- putting toys and activities away and out of sight in solid-colored containers, and
- playing white noise to provide a consistent background sound during rest times and learning activities that require concentration.

Movement games such as Freeze Dance; Red Light, Green Light; and Simon Says provide children with movement input and help them learn self-control. To succeed at these activities, children must pay attention so that they act when they should and stop when they should. When they engage in these fun games, children receive movement input, which helps with their attention and focus. They must also listen, stop, and think about the action they should make before they act. For example, during Freeze Dance, children must remain active listeners and inhibit their motion when the music stops. During Simon Says, they need to listen attentively and only act when the instructor starts the direction with the words "Simon says." Young children need a lot of practice to develop strong inhibitory-control skills. Developing this important executive-function skill with a movement game is an excellent way to motivate all children to participate and learn self-control.

Putting It All Together

Sensory strategies help children focus and sustain an optimal level of arousal during difficult parts of their school day. When children are able to focus, they can access their executive-function skills to remain flexible, remember what they need to, and maintain self-control throughout the day. Sensory strategies are not the only way to support executive functioning in the classroom. In the next chapter, we explore a variety of cognitive strategies and activities to support children's ability to focus, remain flexible, organize their thoughts and actions, and maintain self-control.

Chapter 4:

Cognitive Activities to Improve Executive-Function Skills

Early learning classrooms are excellent environments for nurturing strong executive-function skills. Helping young children develop flexible thinking, working memory, and self-control will not only support them as they learn, play, and socialize with their peers in preschool and kindergarten, but will also create a strong foundation for success. Executive functions are skills people rely on throughout their lives. Children can work on executive-function skills in the classroom by engaging in cognitive activities that indirectly focus on attentional flexibility, working memory, and inhibitory control. These activities allow them to learn through play and teach them metacognition, theory of mind, and time-management skills.

Metacognition

Metacognition is the awareness of one's thought process. It refers to how people think about the way they think. When children are taught to be aware of what they are (or should be) thinking about, they can begin to understand how they think and learn; what things are easy for them; and what challenges they may have with thinking, remembering, or learning. This can be an effective tool for teaching executive-function skills. Teachers can ask children to think about how to remember a task, how they are going to plan and manage an activity, and how they might choose to remain patient when they really want something.

Techniques for teaching children the metacognition skills they'll need to support strong executive functions include cueing them before an activity starts that they will need to use their active listening, memory, and patience skills, and asking them to think about how and when to remember necessary information. Teachers can remind them that listening, remembering, and being patient are important.

To support a young child's metacognition abilities, teach them how to get ready for learning. Tell them which learning strategies they will need, and remind them that they can pay attention, learn, and remember. Before starting a new activity, consider preparing children by talking about what they need to do to be successful in the activity, such as turning on their listening ears and paying attention to the directions so that they can focus, remember, and participate fully in the activity. You can do this by engaging in simple but effective metacognition activities, such as modeling and visualizing.

Model Metacognition

Throughout the school day, model how you think about remembering things, remind yourself to be a flexible thinker, actively listen, and wait patiently. When something comes up, remind the children through your thoughts and actions that everyone can switch gears, try something new, or play a different way. Talking about changes and disruptions when they occur and then demonstrating how to deal with them lets you model flexible thinking and task-switching. Encourage children to talk aloud about their actions before they start an activity. This will not only increase their awareness about their personal thought patterns but may also provide a helpful model for other children in the class.

For example, you may talk with the class about a new activity and state, "Okay, I always seem to forget some of the steps when I do this activity, so I am going to really concentrate on listening to the directions and remembering them so I don't forget anything." Or, at snack time on a rainy, cold day, you can say, "Darn it. I really wanted the class to play outside today. But the weather isn't good, so we are going to have to play in the gym instead." This alerts children that there will be a change in plans before this occurs and models flexible thinking about the change. You could continue to model flexible thinking by talking with the class about what they can do in the gym that they can't do outside.

Visualize Metacognition

Before teaching a new activity, talk with children about how they might think about and focus on the things they need to be successful. Teaching children to think about paying attention and remembering, and then cueing them to actively think about the skills they need before starting an activity, is a useful metacognition strategy that helps them actively access their executive-function skills. The following activity can be used as a tool to help children visualize the senses they use to remember and focus.

Activity: Activating the Senses

Helping children visualize the senses they need to listen and remember can improve active listening and working-memory skills. Young children need to learn that their ears listen and their eyes see, and they must think about these functions in order to be good at them. Additionally, children can learn to "activate" their senses when you cue them that it is time to listen, pay attention, and remember important information. At the start of a new activity, teach children that listening and remembering are important skills and that their eyes, ears, and brain help them with these skills.

Intended Outcomes

- Children will be prepared for active listening before starting an activity.
- Children will actively think about remembering what they need to.
- Children will demonstrate increased awareness of the importance of active listening and remembering.

Materials

Visual of a pair of eyes
Visual of an ear
Visual of a brain

What to Do

1. Show a visual of an ear, and ask the children what they use their ears for. Remind them that they use their ears to listen to directions.
2. Show a visual of a pair of eyes. Ask what they use their eyes for, and remind them that they need to use their eyes to see what they are doing, look for materials, and copy actions.
3. Present the class with a visual of a brain, and ask what they use their brains for. Cue the children that they can use their brains to pay attention to and then remember the steps to complete an activity.

It may take young children a few learning opportunities to remember what the eyes, ears, and brain are for. This is an activity that the teacher can repeat often until everyone in the class understands.

When explaining what classroom learning activities entail, consider using language such as, "Okay, this is important. Time to tell your brain to remember what I am saying." Or, "Time for listening and learning! Let's turn on our listening ears!"

Encourage Metacognitive Self-Awareness

As children's metacognition skills improve, they will learn that self-awareness and self-reflection are important school skills needed for success. Fewer cues will be required to remind them to think about these skills. This is important because with self-awareness comes improved problem-solving, flexible thinking, and self-control skills. Self-aware children are able to manage their metacognitive thoughts by reflecting on questions such as:

- What am I doing right now?
- What is the class doing?
- What is the goal of this activity?
- What do I need to be using to be successful?

Theory of Mind

Theory of mind refers to a person's ability to think about how someone else thinks. Specifically, it is the understanding that other people may have different thoughts and beliefs about something that may cause them to feel and act differently (Kimhi et al., 2014). Theory of mind is important for succeeding in social interactions, understanding and following rules, and achieving attentional flexibility (Chu, 2021). This skill develops over time and with practice.

Preschool-aged children may have just started understanding how they feel about things. Developmentally, they are not able to think about or predict the thoughts and feelings of another person. Prekindergarten-aged children are starting to understand that different people may feel and act differently than they do. By the end of kindergarten, most children should have developed an understanding about their own thoughts and feelings (Kimhi et al., 2014). They are better able to see that others have their own set of thoughts and feelings and that another person may think and act differently. In the following vignette, Mr. Heber introduces the concept of theory of mind as he talks with Ajay, Ricky, and Sarah about how children like to play differently with the dinosaurs at the sand and water table.

> Ajay likes to play rough with the dinosaurs at the sand and water table in his prekindergarten classroom. He likes the dark green T. rex dinosaur and plays with this toy by stomping through the sand and water and roaring at other dinosaur toys. Ricky also likes to play with dinosaurs, but he prefers to make caves for them to sleep in and pathways for them to walk along. Ricky enjoys creating an elaborate play space for the dinosaurs and does not like it when Ajay messes it up. One afternoon during

free choice, Ricky and another child, Sarah, are playing together at the sand and water table. They have worked hard to make a habitat for Ricky's dinosaurs and Sarah's unicorn. Ajay enters the play space, grabs his favorite T. rex, and starts roaring loudly. Sarah shouts, "No, Ajay!" grabs her unicorn out of the sand, and leaves the play space. Ricky also shouts at Ajay and calls over Mr. Heber, the classroom teacher. "Ajay's going to ruin everything," Ricky says. "No, I'm not! My dinosaur just likes to stomp around," Ajay replies. Mr. Heber responds, "Ajay, I know you love to play with the T. rex, but Ricky and Sarah have been working hard to create a habitat in the sand. How do you think they will feel if your T. rex comes in and destroys it all?" Ajay shrugs his shoulders. Mr. Huber continues, "And Ricky, Ajay loves pretending with the T. rex. I think his feelings might be hurt if you don't let him play with you." Ricky replies, "But he's too rough. It's not fun."

Mr. Heber thinks for a moment and says, "Hmm. I wonder what we can do so you can both play dinosaurs together without becoming upset." He waits for the boys to provide suggestions and then helps them see the value of playing together without hurting one another's feelings. Ajay asks if the water part of the table could be for his T. rex to play rough. When Ricky agrees, Ajay continues, "But he is a bad guy and he is going to roar at your dinosaurs." Ricky thinks about this for a moment, smiles, and says, "Okay. What if he is the bad guy, and he's trying to come into my territory and steal all of our things, and I have to keep him out by building a huge electric fence around the habitat?" Both boys are happy with their compromise and play together until free-play time ends.

While theory of mind is a difficult concept for young children to grasp, it is possible for them to learn that not everyone thinks the way they do, and not everyone acts the way they do. Teaching theory of mind supports both attentional flexibility and inhibitory-control skills. In the example, Ajay understood that Ricky had worked hard at building a habitat for the dinosaurs and didn't like it when Ajay's dinosaur smashed and destroyed it. He thought of a new way to play so both boys could have fun together. This shows both flexible thinking and self-control. Ajay controlled his desire to destroy the habitat and was flexible when he chose a different way to play. Engaging in activities that require children to think about another person's point of view while at school will help them improve their theory-of-mind skills.

Activity: Profession Role-Play

Role-play is an excellent activity to help children learn to think about the perspective of another person. By pretending to do a specific job that they have some knowledge about, such as a chef, teacher, or veterinarian, they are better able to understand how someone else might act.

Intended Outcomes

- Children will think about and act out the perspective of another person.
- Children will improve flexible thinking as they role-play scenarios with classmates or caregivers.
- Children will develop theory-of-mind skills.

Materials

Dress-up clothes (doctor, veterinarian, construction worker, teacher, and chef are common options)

Tools and props for each profession (doctor's kit, thermometer, construction tools, cooking utensils, and so on)

Visuals that demonstrate jobs and careers

What to Do

1. Make sure at least two people are willing to role-play.
2. Support the children in choosing what they'd like to pretend to be.
3. Once they've decided, encourage them to dress up like that person.

4. Ask the children to gather the materials they'll need. Have visuals available to depict the tools people need to perform specific jobs.

5. Support the children's role-playing by reminding them of their new roles. Give them tips and suggestions if they begin to feel stuck. For example, if a child is pretending to be a chef, state, "I think some of your customers are hungry. Can you cook them some food?" If a child is pretending to be a veterinarian, bring over a stuffed animal and say, "I think this animal is sick. Can you give it a checkup to find out what's wrong?"

Activity: Reading and Predicting What Might Happen Next

Reading books aloud during circle time or in small groups is a great way to work on developing children's theory-of-mind skills. By predicting what might happen next and discussing characters' emotions and actions, children learn to think about the characters' perspectives.

Intended Outcomes

- Children will improve theory-of-mind skills.
- Children will improve their ability to think about another person's perspective.
- Children will improve their ability to think about and predict what happens next.
- Children will improve active-listening skills.

Materials

Highly engaging books such as:

Duck, Duck, Moose by Mary Sullivan
We're Going on a Bear Hunt by Michael Rosen
Go Away, Big Green Monster by Ed Emberley
Leonardo the Terrible Monster by Mo Willems
Elephant and Piggie books by Mo Willems

Ricky, the Rock That Couldn't Roll by Mr. Jay
Cats Don't Like That! by Andy Wortlock

What to Do

1. One-on-one, in a small group, or during circle time, read a highly engaging book to children, stopping often to ask questions about the characters' thoughts and actions.
2. Pause occasionally to ask them to think about what might happen next.
3. Talk with children about why characters respond or feel the way they do.
4. Ask children what they might do in a similar situation.

Time Management

Time management supports strong executive-function skills and is an important school skill, even in the preschool classroom (Michel and Bimmüller, 2023). When children can manage their time well, they exhibit more self-control and transition skills. Strong time-management skills help decrease challenging behaviors, such as task abandonment, avoidance, frustration, and impulsivity. They also support self-control. To help children develop time-management skills, teach them the concept of time and provide visuals to support time management.

Teach the Concept of Time

Understanding the concept of time will help children better understand time management and how time passes during the school day. By using visual supports and time-based language, children can learn how to conceptualize the school day and its activities. This helps with patience, self-control, transitioning, sticking with and completing tasks, and flexible thinking skills.

Labeling parts of the day as free-play time, circle time, center time, and so on encourages children to recognize what part of the day it is. Supports such as visual timers, sand timers, and visual schedules further help children manage and understand time so that they complete activities within a given time frame, transition when they need to, and remain patient as they wait for something they want to happen.

Provide Visuals to Support Time Management

Because they haven't learned how to tell time yet, a visual representation of time passing shows children how long they need to wait for something, how much time they have left for an activity, or when an activity they are looking forward to, such as lunch or outdoor play, will happen. The better children are at managing their time independently, the easier it will be to access and rely on their executive-function skills. Visual supports help with flexible thinking and self-control as children use the supports to remain patient, transition on time, and complete activities independently.

A visual timer helps children begin to grasp how time passes. Unlike a clock, a visual timer shows time passing with a colored disc. As time passes, the colors disappear, and when the time is up, all of the color is gone. Using a visual timer during centers and other times when children might need to demonstrate self-control and patience shows them how long they have to wait and also assures them that their turn is coming up soon. This type of time-management support helps children independently manage their work and may motivate them to stay on task to complete what they are working on.

A visual schedule defines for the class the flow and organization of the day. It is a combination of pictures and words that helps children visualize what will happen and in what order. Place the visual schedule in a consistent spot in the classroom that is easy for children to see. That way, when they wonder when snack time is or when it will be free time, they can understand how long they need to wait. This time-management skill supports patience and self-control.

Teachers can also use a visual schedule to show a change or disruption to the usual routine, such as a guest coming in to talk with the class or a field trip. Talking about these changes before they occur and allowing children to visualize when they will happen supports attentional flexibility and flexible thinking.

A sand timer visually shows children the passage of time. It is a tool that individual children can use to manage their time when they are wondering when an activity will end or how long they have to wait until it is their turn for something. Sand timers are available in a variety of colors and have time intervals that range from one to thirty minutes.

Use an Analog Clock

Unlike digital clocks, analog clocks show time passing by the second, minute, and hour. Although young children are not yet able to tell time, referring to the analog clock throughout the day shows them that time is passing. Teachers can demonstrate one minute passing on the second hand and can reference the minute and hour hands to help children recognize that time passes and that, at different parts of the day, different events and activities occur.

Young children can learn time concepts such as:

- Day and night
- Morning, afternoon, and nighttime
- Past, present, and future
- Winter, spring, summer, and fall
- Day, week, month, and year
- Second, minute, and hour

Teach these concepts during circle time or as a small-group activity. The following activities help teach the concept of time.

Activity: How Long Does It Take?

In small groups or as a class, explore the concept of time by learning how long it takes to complete a task or activity. For example, how long does it take to walk from one side of the classroom to the other? How long does it take to walk to the end of the hallway? How long does it take to walk to the playground?

Intended Outcomes

- Children will learn the concept of time.
- Children will learn the concept of time passing.
- Children will become aware of seconds and minutes.

Materials

Stopwatch or timer
Paper and writing utensil to record times (optional)

What to Do

1. Talk with children about time as it relates to how long it takes to do various tasks, duties, or play activities. For example, it takes a long time to cook a meal, but it takes just a few seconds to take a sip of milk. It takes a long time to drive to the store but just a few minutes to walk out to the playground.

2. Let children know that they are going to use a stopwatch (or timer) to observe how long it takes to get to places around the school. Allow children to offer suggestions for places they'd like to walk to.

3. Choose locations around the school that are very close (perhaps from one side of the classroom to the other) and far away so that children can compare time and distance.

4. Ask children to guess how long they think it will take to walk to the places they have chosen, and record their guesses.

5. Line up the group, remind everyone the rules about body safety and walking, start the timer, and walk to the destination.

6. Stop the timer, announce how long it took to arrive at the destination, and record the time.

7. Talk about time in terms of seconds and minutes and long distance and short distance.

Activity: What Is It Time For?

This game has endless possibilities to help children understand the concept of time. It may be played as a visualization activity or by using visual aids.

Intended Outcomes

- Children will learn the concept of time.
- Children will learn that different activities happen at different times of the day.
- Children will learn that the weather changes over the course of a month or a year.

Materials

Optional visual aids: website, photos, books

What to Do

1. Before playing this game, decide what concept you will teach and whether children will visualize the concept in their heads or look at visuals to help guide them through the activity. Possible concepts to teach include the seasons and the time of the day.

2. Gather children in a small group, or do the activity during circle time.

3. Let the group know that they will be learning about the concept chosen ahead of time by playing "What Is It Time For?"

4. Describe a scenario. For example, if the time concept you are teaching relates to the time of day, then possible scenarios might be the following:

    - "You've been at school all morning and you're getting hungry. What is it time for?" (Possible answers to this question: snack time or lunchtime)
    - "We've been learning inside the classroom all day. Our bodies are getting wiggly, and we need to get out some energy. What is it time for?" (Possible answers: recess time, play time, or outside time)
    - "It's dark outside and you're starting to get sleepy. What is it time for?" (bedtime)

5. Allow plenty of time for children to think of possible answers on their own. If the class struggles to state a reasonable answer, provide hints and clues to move the game along.

Activity: What Time Is It, Mr. Fox?

This is a fun movement game that helps children think about time while also working on listening, focusing, and patience. The game can be played outside or in a large, open, indoor space such as the gym.

Intended Outcomes

- Children will practice counting skills.
- Children will think about time and the concept of time.
- Children will learn patience and active-listening skills while they wait and respond as directed.

Materials

None

What to Do

What Time Is It, Mr. Fox? is a game of tag but with a twist. The point of the game is to walk or step past the person who is acting as Mr. Fox without getting tagged.

1. Choose a person to be Mr. or Mrs. Fox. (For the first few rounds, it is a good idea for Mr. Fox to be an adult so children can learn how to play the game correctly.)
2. Ask the children to form a straight line.
3. Ask Mr. Fox to stand at least ten to fifteen feet away from the children.
4. All at one time, they will ask, "What time is it, Mr. Fox?"
5. The fox will reply with an hour of the day such as, "It's three o'clock!"
6. Children will take as many steps forward as the time Mr. Fox has called out. They can take any sized step they like. Some children will want to get close to the fox as quickly as possible while others will want to lag behind and take smaller steps.
7. Children will continue to ask what time it is, and the fox will continue to answer with a time of the day, until Mr. Fox decides to call out, "Lunchtime!" This indicates that the fox is going to run and chase them, trying to tag them out of the game. To stay in the game, children must get to the fox before he calls out *lunchtime* or must run back to the start line without getting tagged.

Modifications to the game:

- Once a person is tagged, they can become the fox.
- The fox can face the children or have their back to the children until they call out "Lunchtime!"
- If young children find *lunchtime* too scary, the phrase can be replaced with a different word. Children can freeze in place if they are tagged and then become a helper to Mr. Fox for future rounds until there is just one child who remains untagged.

Putting It All Together

Cognitive strategies teach children to think about how they think, which allows them to take an active role in their learning, listen on purpose, and remember what they need to. When children are able to see a situation from another person's perspective, they learn the importance of flexible thinking, self-control, and patience. Finally, when children understand the concept of time and how time passes, they are better able to manage their own time independently, complete activities in a timely manner, and be more patient. In the next chapter, we explore different play strategies and activities that nurture and support executive functions.

Chapter 5:
Play Activities to Improve Executive-Function Skills

One of the best ways to help children develop strong executive-function skills is to practice using these skills when children do not need them. As children improve their skills during play, they retain the abilities and can start to apply the skills in other parts of the school day. Through play, children become more flexible in their thinking, improve problem-solving skills, and work on self-control. Play also helps children gain perspective, follow and remember directions, and develop social skills. Three types of play help foster strong executive function and can be incorporated into the school day in early learning classrooms: open-ended, unstructured play; role-play; and pretend and imaginary play.

Open-Ended Play

In open-ended play, children engage with games and materials how they'd like, with no expected outcome or specific finished product. This is a time when children can explore learning materials, sensory inputs, and toys. They may learn to scoop and pour at a sand and water table. They may dig a giant hole on the playground. Or they might build an elaborate city from blocks or cardboard boxes. While engaged in open-ended play, children learn problem-solving, flexible thinking, and self-control as well as strengthen working-memory skills. With practice and metacognitive thinking, children can transfer these skills to other parts of the school day.

Open-ended play also helps children develop mindfulness skills, work on impulse control, decrease behavioral outbursts, and improve social interactions.

Just because the play is unstructured doesn't mean teachers have no control over the activity. They may arrange unstructured play activities to include items related to a theme the class is learning about or a motor skill the children need to practice. For example, if children are having difficulty feeding themselves neatly, put spoons, forks, bowls, and cups in the sensory table. When children play in this space, they practice scooping, pouring, and using utensils while also developing patience, social skills, working memory, and flexible thinking.

Organizing Open-Ended Play Experiences

To ensure a positive outcome, teachers must set up open-ended play spaces or activities well. First, take time to organize open-ended play opportunities for children. Will they play in small groups seated at a table? Will they engage in open-ended play at a sensory table or other center station?

Next, decide if there is a specific set of skills the class could work on improving. This might include buttoning, zippering, and lacing; utensil use; building and constructing; or messy play. The activity might complement a theme the class is learning about, such as the four seasons, reptiles, plants, or transportation. Set up the activity so that children have specific materials to engage with to support these skills or themes.

Finally, set a timer and allow children to play with the materials as they see fit.

Consider providing suggestions to support children who may struggle to get started with open-ended play. Model ways to use the materials and encourage children to play either cooperatively or in parallel. It is important that children are not told what to do, as the purpose of unstructured play is for them to use their imaginations.

Using Natural Objects

The possibilities for play with objects found in nature are endless. Natural objects such as sand, pinecones, rocks, and leaves evoke a sense of wonder. Playing with them at the sensory table or creating art projects with them while seated in a small group will help children learn to be flexible thinkers, share limited resources, and gain self-control. Children may also interact directly with nature while playing outside in a wooded area or a sandbox filled with natural objects. The following activities demonstrate how children may interact with natural objects through exploratory play. These activities also support attentional flexibility, self-control, time management, and working-memory skills.

Activity: Exploring Natural Materials at the Sensory Table or Sensory Tray

Intended Outcomes

- Children will interact imaginatively with objects found in nature.
- Children will improve attentional flexibility as they play with natural items in new ways.
- Children will work on self-control as they share limited resources and interact with peers at the sensory table or sensory tray.

Materials

Objects found in nature
Sand, pebbles, shredded paper, or packaging material
Tools such as small brushes, spoons, and bowls

What to Do

1. Fill the sensory table or tray with a base. Possibilities include sand, shredded paper, pebbles, and packaging material.

2. Add in the natural objects, such as items children find while out on a nature walk or those a teacher brings into the class.

3. Add other objects to aid in exploration, such as small brushes, spoons, and bowls.
4. During centers or free-choice time, encourage children to explore the materials at the sensory table or tray.

Note: Children may need encouragement to play and explore in this space because it is an especially unstructured form of open-ended play. Suggest that they're archaeologists searching the sensory table for precious objects or that they are on a scavenger hunt.

Activity: Open-Ended Play with Recycled Materials

Recycled materials are an excellent medium for open-ended play. These materials are abundant, free, and have endless possibilities for play. It doesn't matter whether children put multiple cardboard boxes together to create cars, boats, or houses, or whether they simply play with the materials themselves, such as by pretending a paper towel roll is a telescope or a large box is a car. What is important is that they are engaging with the materials and their classmates while having fun and improving their executive-function skills.

Intended Outcomes

- Children will interact imaginatively with recycled materials.
- Children will improve STEM skills as they build and construct.
- Children will work on time management and task completion.
- Children will improve attentional flexibility as they play in new ways with different materials.
- Children will work on self-control as they share limited resources and interact with peers.

Materials

Recycled materials, such as paper-towel rolls, cardboard boxes, and plastic lids
Googly eyes, chenille stems, pompoms

Glue
Child-safe scissors
Duct or masking tape
Colorful fabric
Markers, paint, and paintbrushes

What to Do

1. Collect a variety of recycled materials. Consider asking families or local businesses to donate items.
2. Provide visuals or physical models of possibilities to help children develop their own ideas. Because this is an unstructured and open-ended activity, you'll need to spur children's creativity to get started, plan out materials, and organize their thoughts to create what they are interested in. If a child is stuck for an idea, a favorite children's book may spark their imagination.
3. Tell children that they will be making something of their choosing with the recycled materials and that they can make anything they want by gluing, taping, and coloring boxes.
4. Give ample time for children to collect their materials and start creating. Some children may need encouragement at this point to think up an idea.
5. Set a timer when there are 5 minutes left so children know how much time they have to finish.
6. Display children's creations around the room and compliment their creativity and great ideas!

Activity: Open-Ended Messy Tactile Play

Messy tactile play involves engaging with materials, such as fingerpaint, shaving cream, slime, or sand. Engaging in messy play supports children's executive-function skills as they practice sharing, self-control, and flexible thinking.

Intended Outcomes

- Children will work on flexible thinking skills as they interact with messy materials.
- Children will share limited resources, improving patience and self-control.
- Children will play and interact as they choose with messy materials.

Materials

Trays (one per child)
Messy materials, such as playdough, shaving cream, modeling clay, and fingerpaint
Add-ins to enhance play, such as marbles, toy vehicles, and toy animals

What to Do

1. Invite children to sit in a small group at a table, and set up stations for each child. The stations should include a tray with the messy tactile material already on it. Place add-ins such as small toys, vehicles, or animals in the center of the table so that any child can engage with them.

2. Encourage the children to interact with the materials as they choose. They might draw shapes and lines with their fingers, drive cars or roll marbles around the tray, or build imaginary habitats for the plastic animals.

3. Set a timer when there are 5 minutes left so children know how much time they have left to play.

Note: Some children may not want to touch messy materials. Those children can use brushes or spoons to interact with the material until they feel comfortable.

Note: This may be a highly desired activity for the class. Children who aren't playing at this station may need support, such as timers, to wait patiently for their turn.

Role-Play

Role-play, which is when a child assumes another person's or character's role, requires some understanding of theory of mind and metacognition. Children must think about acting and responding the way another person would, rather than the way they would. With practice and some prompting, it is a type of play that even preschool children can engage in. However, most three- to five-year-old children will need the support of an adult to remind them of their role and to prompt them as needed.

Role-play is useful in helping children work through things that are difficult for them, such as waiting their turn and listening to teachers when they are talking. This type of play supports theory of mind because it allows children to understand a situation from another person's point of view. It also supports children's attentional flexibility and perspective-taking, as they can act out daily life experiences through play to learn different strategies for navigating challenging situations that arise during the school day. These next activities provide ways to incorporate role-play into the classroom to support perspective-taking, flexible thinking, self-control, and working-memory skills.

Activity: Role Reversal

In this activity, children become the teacher. This is especially helpful for teaching specific executive-function skills that children may be struggling with in the classroom, such as sitting still, not talking over the teacher, or not blurting out answers without waiting their turn. The child runs a mock circle-time experience while the teacher acts similarly to the child, making sounds, not paying attention, and so on.

Intended Outcomes

- Children will develop theory-of-mind skills as they take on the role of the teacher.

- Children will learn the importance of self-control.
- Children will practice working-memory skills to recall the situation they are acting out.

Materials

Optional materials might include items the teacher uses often, such as a pointer or talking stick

What to Do

1. Talk with the child or children who will be role-playing with you about what role-play is. Explain that they will act like the teacher while you pretend to be a child.
2. Answer children's questions and remind them of the parts of the activity they will be acting out.
3. Begin the role-play activity. Use props to make the simulation seem true to life.
4. At the end of the activity, talk with the children about how they think it went. Ask questions about their thoughts, feelings, and actions.
5. Encourage children to think about how they might act in a real situation like the one they just acted out.

Activity: Role-Play for Challenging Events

Together as a class, children role-play through challenging situations that sometimes arise at school. Typical challenging situations might include:

- responding to an unexpected fire drill,
- asking to play with a group of children on the playground,
- sharing limited resources, and
- asking for help when something is hard.

Intended Outcomes

- Children will learn strategies to manage challenging situations.
- Children will learn flexible thinking as they consider different ways of reacting to challenging situations.
- Children will learn perspective-taking as they listen to and consider the thoughts and ideas of their classmates.

Materials

None

What to Do

1. Decide on the challenging situation that you and the children will role-play.
2. Gather the children as a group and describe the situation. For example, if role-playing what to do when the fire alarm goes off, describe for children a time when your child-care center or school carried out a fire drill.
3. Ask children how they feel in the situation. For example, "How do you feel when you are playing quietly and suddenly the fire alarm goes off?"
4. Allow time for children to describe how they feel when this happens.
5. Spend time processing these feelings as a class. Some children might state that they feel scared. Others might feel mad that they have to stop playing. And others may say they aren't bothered by the drill.
6. Ask the class what they should do when they hear the alarm go off, reminding them that it is okay to feel scared, mad, and frustrated. Possible responses might include, "We stop what we are doing and line up," "We go outside," and "We cover our ears."
7. Role-play the challenging situation with the children. Tell them they will be acting out what to do the next time the challenging event

occurs. Answer any questions they have before beginning. For example, when role-playing for a fire drill, begin by having children pretend to be occupied by an activity. Then a "fire alarm" sounds, with the teacher making a loud sound with her voice or setting off a timer on her phone. Children will act out stopping what they are doing, lining up at the door, and walking out of the building.

8. When the role-play has concluded, gather the class again to talk about what went well and answer any questions. Praise children for a job well done! Then, the next time a real fire drill occurs, remind them what they learned and practiced during the simulation.

Pretend and Imaginary Play

Pretend play is when children copy the actions of a familiar job or scenario like playing house, school, or restaurant. They mimic a scenario they have observed before and take on the roles of the people involved. Preschool children may be able to pretend play only in parallel with one another, but by the end of the prekindergarten year, most children should have the ability to pretend play cooperatively with their peers. Creating a pretend-play area in an early learning classroom is a wonderful space for children to play together, learn to be flexible thinkers, share limited resources, and improve working-memory skills.

Imaginary play is when children invent a unique scenario that evolves as the play progresses. It allows children to be anything or anyone—a dinosaur or a kitten, an astronaut or a superhero—and imagine where they are playing: a swamp, a forest, outer space, or a made-up world. This is the most sophisticated type of play because it requires a great deal of creative thought and flexible thinking. Imaginary play may be difficult for three- and even some four-year-olds to engage in, especially in cooperation with classmates.

Because young children will have limited imaginary-play skills, they may be limited to just acting out the role of an animal or person. Preschool children think in concrete ways, so they may need realistic props in their imaginary-play world. For example, a three-year-old may put on a chef's hat and try to "cook" a meal using plastic food and utensils. A kindergarten child pretending to be a chef may make food out of playdough or clay, as their pretend-play abilities are more mature. Older children may be able to develop more elaborate imaginary play sequences and to replace common objects to fit their needs. For example, a wooden stick could serve as a wand, or a rock could serve as a dinosaur egg.

The following activities provide suggestions for incorporating imaginary play activities into the classroom to support perspective-taking, working memory, flexible thinking, task switching, self-control, and problem-solving skills.

Activity: Dress for Success

Intended Outcomes

- Children will learn flexible thinking as they engage in pretend play with their classmates.
- Children will practice working-memory skills as they remember their roles and the roles of their peers.
- Children will learn problem-solving skills as they act out pretend-play scenarios.
- Children will learn perspective-taking and theory-of-mind skills.

Materials

Toys, props, and clothing related to different jobs. These may be homemade or store-bought depending on time and resources.

Possible materials to support being a veterinarian or doctor:

- Stuffed animals
- Toy doctor kit (stethoscope, tongue depressor, plastic syringe, pill bottle)
- Lab coat

- Name tag
- Clipboard
- Bandages, tissue paper, or white paper to act as bandages for injuries
- Toy bed or cardboard box for examination table

Possible materials to support being an explorer:

- Sun hat
- Vest full of pockets
- Toy camera
- Binoculars or telescope (plastic or made from paper-towel rolls)
- Magnifying glass
- Compass

Possible materials to support being a chef or playing restaurant or grocery store:

- Plastic food
- Empty food boxes
- Play money
- Utensils and dishes
- Pots and pans
- Pad of paper and writing utensils to take orders
- Menus
- Chef hat
- Apron
- Calculator or toy cash register

Possible materials to support being a pilot, police officer, or firefighter:

- Dress-up clothes
- Sunglasses
- Badges

What to Do

If the pretend-play space is organized, children should be able to play on their own with little adult guidance. That said, they may need help putting on dress-up clothes or working through conflict. Set up for success!

1. Designate a space in the classroom for pretend play.
2. Hang dress-up clothes on hooks or a child-sized coat tree so children can easily see the dress-up options.
3. Place accompanying props and toys in a bin with a photograph of the vocation.
4. Set a timer at the start of pretend-play time. This will support children's time management and transitions. This area may be a popular one for children.
5. Encourage children to put toys and props in the correct bins during cleanup time so that the next group of children can easily find what they want.

Activity: Imagination Station

Similar to dressing up and acting out different jobs, the imagination station lets children dress up and pretend to be somebody or something else. The difference is that they can pretend to be a fairy-tale character, superhero, animal, or mythical creature. This requires more creative thinking, working memory, and cooperation. While dreaming up unique ways to play, children will work on self-control and flexible thinking.

Intended Outcomes

- Children will learn flexible thinking as they engage in pretend play with their classmates.
- Children will develop working-memory skills as they remember their role and those of their peers.

- Children will learn problem-solving skills as they act out pretend-play scenarios.
- Children will learn perspective-taking and theory-of-mind skills.

Materials

Superhero capes
Tutus
Wearable wings
Scarves or pretty fabric
Pretend animal tails or ears
Hats, plastic crowns, and plastic tiaras
Purses or pretty bags
Wands

What to Do

As with the pretend-play space, organize the imagination station to allow children to imagine play scenarios on their own, but be ready to provide help as needed. You can house the imagination station with other dress-up clothes or in the pretend-play area of the classroom if one already exists.

1. Place a sign that says "Imagination Station" on a large plastic bin or laundry basket, and put all the clothes, props, and toys in the bin.
2. Allow children to go through the bin and use any item they want as they pretend to be a mythical being, a kitty queen, a flying puppy, a superhero, or another role.
3. Encourage cooperative play, regardless of what children pretend to be.
4. Emphasize that the imagination station is for creativity, thinking up new worlds, and having fantastic experiences.
5. When there are five minutes left to play, set a timer to help children with time management and transitions.

6. Encourage children to place all items back in the imagination station bin when cleaning up.

Putting It All Together

During play, children have the opportunity to learn and develop executive-function skills. With guidance from teachers and caregivers, they can use these skills during other parts of their day. Through play, children learn to be more flexible thinkers, remember story sequences and the rules of games they've made up, and exercise self-control as they interact with their friends and classmates. In the next chapter, we examine additional classroom activities that help improve children's executive-function skills.

Chapter 6:

Classroom Activities to Improve Executive-Function Skills

Children rely on their executive-function skills to learn, play, and socialize throughout the school day. These skills help them attend to what they should, filter out what is irrelevant, remember the parts required to complete an activity, and then carry out the tasks in the correct order. Children use executive-function skills during play and learning activities to set a goal, remember and plan the steps needed, and then sustain their attention until the activity is complete. Engaging in classroom activities that improve attentional flexibility, working memory, and inhibitory control will have a positive effect on child success, as children with strong executive-function skills are better at learning and retaining information, socializing, and managing their thoughts and emotions.

There are many games and activities geared toward early learners that, with a bit of modification and guidance, can directly address working memory, inhibitory control, and attentional flexibility. Playing these games and engaging in these activities often will improve executive-function skills and provide children with strategies they can use when they run into a challenging situation during other parts of the school day. The more executive-function skills are practiced and talked about, the stronger those skills will be. In this chapter, you'll find games and activities commonly used in an early childhood environment—but with a few modifications so that children are strengthening their executive-function skills while having fun.

Classroom Activities to Improve Attentional Flexibility

Children rely on attentional flexibility throughout the school day as they react to changes and disruptions to the usual routine, such as when friends are absent from school, when favorite toys go missing, or when teachers introduce new activities. Games and activities that require children to switch from one activity to another and think in flexible ways help them improve their attentional flexibility skills. The following games and activities will support children in developing these skills so that when a disruption occurs or when something does not go their way, children are able to shift gears and adapt to the change.

Activity: Bingo (Letters or Numbers)

Bingo requires all three executive-function skills, as children need to actively listen and remember the numbers or letters called. They need to practice self-control as they mark off only the items called out. Playing bingo in different ways is an excellent way to help children learn task-switching and flexible thinking. For example, the winner may need to get five in a row in one round and have the whole board covered in a different round.

Intended Outcomes

- Children will learn that there is more than one way to play a game.
- Children will improve flexible-thinking skills.
- Children will practice task-switching skills.
- Children will improve working-memory and active-listening skills.
- Children will practice inhibitory-control skills.
- Children will work on letter and/or number identification.

Materials

Bingo game boards

Place markers, such as colored plastic discs, coins, small rocks, ripped pieces of paper, or dry erase markers if using laminated game boards

Alphabet letters, numbers, colors, or animal cards that correspond to the items on the game boards

What to Do

Decide which game board will be best for the class. You can purchase bingo kits or download customized game boards online, including game boards made up of colors, letters, numbers, and animals. As each child will need to mark the game boards in some way, choose a marker that is right for the class.

1. Give one game board and a handful of markers to each child.
2. Explain the rules, giving an example of what to do when an item is called out.
3. Decide on how a child will win a round, either by filling the whole board if there are few items or by completing a row.
4. Show children how they win a round, and demonstrate what winning looks like.
5. Begin calling out items and helping children mark them off on their game board as needed.
6. The round ends when a child calls out, "Bingo!" and has covered the correct items.

Activity: Can We Do It a Different Way?

This activity can occur in small or large groups. The idea is to think of a common task or activity, then come up with a way to do it differently. Once children understand how to do this activity, they can regularly apply the concept throughout the year to help them with flexible thinking when they get stuck on doing something or playing in just one way.

Intended Outcomes

- Children will improve flexible thinking.
- Children will improve task-switching skills.
- Children will learn that there is more than one way to do things.

Materials

None

What to Do

1. Before playing this game with children, think of a few things in the classroom or on the school grounds that can be done in different ways. For example, there might be multiple ways to walk to the playground or to water the class plants.

2. Gather children in a small group, or do the activity during circle time.

3. Let the group know that you are going to challenge them to think up new and different ways to do the things they always do.

4. To get the game started, describe a scenario. For example: "In our class, we always water the plants with the watering can. How can we do it a different way?" Possible answers include using a cup or a spray bottle. Or, "We always walk to the playground by going down the main hall and out the side doors. How can we do it a different way?" Possible answers depend on the layout of the school.

5. Once children understand the game, see if anyone has other ideas, and think up scenarios based on what they suggest.

Educators and children can apply this concept when a disruption to the normal routine occurs. For example, if a guest speaker is scheduled to visit, which will disrupt the typical morning schedule, say, "We always have free time, then centers, then snack. If we have a guest speaker come in to talk with us this morning, how can we do our routine differently?"

Activity: What Else Can It Be?

This activity can occur in small or large groups. Once children understand what to do, apply this concept throughout the year to help children with flexible thinking when they get stuck on doing something or playing in just one way. The items children use will demonstrate that most things have more than one use.

Intended Outcomes

- Children will learn that items can have more than one use.
- Children will improve flexible-thinking skills.
- Children will improve task-switching skills.

Materials

Items that can be used for a new purpose, such as:

- Paper-towel roll (telescope, musical instrument, rocket ship)
- Rock (doorstop, paperweight, part of an art project)
- Dishcloth or towel (blindfold, bandage, blanket)

What to Do

1. Gather children in a small group, or do the activity during circle time.
2. Let the group know that they are going to think up new and different ways to use ordinary objects.
3. Present the class with a familiar object, and either describe how it is typically used or ask children to suggest its use.
4. Ask what else the object might be used for. For example, a dishcloth is used to wipe up spills and to dry things, but it can also be used as a blindfold, a blanket to wrap a doll or stuffie in, or even a bandage when playing veterinarian or hospital.

Activity: Circle-Time Read-Aloud

Reading books with characters who are inflexible thinkers is a great way to talk with children about the importance of attentional flexibility. Talking about the characters' actions and feelings, predicting what will happen next, and discussing different ways characters could have acted and reacted teach children how to be flexible thinkers themselves.

Intended Outcomes

- Children will recognize the difficulties inflexible thinking might cause.
- Children will improve flexible-thinking skills.
- Children will improve task-switching skills.

Materials

Children's books with inflexible thinkers as characters, such as:

Ricky, the Rock That Couldn't Roll by Mr. Jay
Amelia Bedelia's First Day of School by Herman Parish
Spring Stinks: A Little Bruce Book by Ryan T. Higgins

What to Do

1. Choose a book with flexible and inflexible thinkers who are relatable to the age and population of the class. Characters may be human, animal, or mythical. Most children enjoy listening to books about conflict and problems. Many of these types of books have characters who demonstrate inflexible thinking.
2. Gather children in a small group, or read to them as an activity during circle time.
3. Pause frequently to discuss what is happening in the story. Ask the children questions about how the characters are feeling, what they think about the characters' actions and choices, or what they think might happen next.

4. At the end of the book, talk about what the characters might have done differently and why. Encourage children to suggest ideas. Stress the importance of being a flexible thinker!

Classroom Activities to Improve Working Memory

Children need working-memory skills to successfully engage in cognitive tasks and classroom activities. Activities that support working memory include visualization games, games that require visual memory, sequencing games, and metacognition games. The following games and activities will help children improve their working-memory skills in fun and effective ways.

Activity: What Am I Forgetting?

This is an active-listening activity that helps children with working memory and can be adapted to suit any situation. Think of a situation or routine most children in the class are familiar with, such as getting ready in the morning, getting ready for bed, or setting the table. Go over the routine with the children, and leave something out. For example, when setting the table, a person puts out plates, bowls, cups, utensils, and napkins. Describe the scene in detail, but leave one item out. Encourage children to remember what's been said and to think about what might be missing.

Playing this game regularly will help children with working memory, and over time the skills they learn can be generalized to other classroom activities. Remind the children to think about the activity and the materials they need. Then, they can ask themselves (or be cued by a teacher), "What am I forgetting?"

Intended Outcomes

- Children will work on active-listening skills.
- Children will develop working-memory skills.
- Children will recognize the importance of remembering everything that's needed to complete tasks and activities.

Materials

Optional visuals to support the routine being discussed

What to Do

1. Gather children as a large group, and ask them to sit comfortably because they will be engaging in a visualization activity. Tell them that they will need to listen and use their brains to think up possible answers.
2. Explain that you will describe a well-known activity or routine but that something will be missing.
3. Let children know that it is their job to think about what has been forgotten.
4. Describe a familar activity or routine that requires multiple items and leave one out. For example: "It's time to get ready for school! I've brushed my teeth and my hair. I ate breakfast. I have on my clothes and my shoes. What am I forgetting?" Possible answers might be lunch, backpack, or jacket.
5. "I'm helping set the table for dinner. I put out plates, napkins, and a spoon and fork for everyone. What am I forgetting?" Possible answers might be cups, food, or water.
6. Restate the list of items when needed if children struggle to remember what's already been listed.

Repeat this activity often so that children get good at making mental lists. Then, when it's time to remember the steps to complete an activity or the materials that they need, they may be better at recalling.

Activity: My Hands Can See!

For this activity, children use visualization and *stereognosis,* which is the ability to perceive a shape or form using only the sense of touch. This activity indirectly helps with working-memory skills, as children must guess the correct object without being able to see the items.

Intended Outcomes

- Children will work on visualizing.
- Children will practice identifying objects using only the sense of touch.

Materials

Empty tissue box (decorating the box is optional)

Items to place in the tissue box, such as:

- Toy car or train
- Wooden block
- Large pompom
- Plastic animal or bug
- Crayon

Printed photographs of the items hidden in the box

Alternative: Purchase the game *What's in Ned's Head?* for this activity instead of making it yourself.

What to Do

1. Gather children in a small group.
2. Explain that they will find objects using only their sense of touch.
3. Place three to six objects (the specific number depends on the children's ages) in an empty tissue box by putting each item through the opening. (**Note:** These items should be objects found throughout the classroom and should differ greatly in color, texture, and style.)
4. Place the corresponding photographs in plain sight for each child in the group to see.
5. Invite the first child to choose a photograph, place his or her hand in the box, and feel each item carefully until the child has located the object that matches the photo.
6. Once the child finds the correct item, he or she replaces it in the box.
7. Repeat these steps until every child in the group has had a turn.

To make this activity more challenging, have children guess what they are touching without the accompanying photo cards.

To make this activity easier, use items that feel different from one another, such as a plastic starfish, a small rubber ball, and a pencil.

Play this game regularly, switching out the items in the box to keep it fun and exciting.

Consider using items that match class themes.

Activity: What's Missing?

For this activity, children will be presented with three to six items, such as a toy bus, a blue crayon, a ball, and a plastic bear. They will have time to memorize the objects before they are hidden. Children will use visual-memory skills to recall what the items are. Once children are good at that activity, you can modify the game so that one item is removed from the group.

Intended Outcomes

- Children will improve working-memory skills.
- Children will improve visual-memory skills.

Materials

Cloth
Three to six different objects

What to Do

1. Gather children in either a small or large group. This game works well with both sizes as either a center or circle-time activity.
2. Explain that they will look at a group of objects, trying to remember each one.
3. Place three to six objects (depending on the age of the class) on a table as a center activity or on the carpet as a circle-time activity.
4. Give children a minute or two to observe and remember each object.
5. During this time, talk about and label each item, but emphasize that the children should not touch or move them. It is important that the objects do not move once they've been placed on the floor or table.
6. Cover the items with a cloth.
7. Ask children to list the items.
8. Lift the cloth to reveal the objects once every item has been recalled.

Modification

1. Place three to six objects on the table or carpet.
2. Give children a minute or two to memorize what is there.
3. Cover the group of objects with a cloth, and remove one of the items.
4. Lift the cloth to reveal the set of objects, and ask the class which item is missing.

Classroom Activities to Support Inhibitory Control

Inhibitory control is responsible for repressing inappropriate thoughts or actions and responding in a way that matches the task, activity, or social situation. Activities that support inhibitory control include those that require patience and active listening to know when to respond. For example, when playing the game Red Light, Green Light, children must remain patient and listen actively, responding only when the game leader calls out, "Green light." When children practice these skills, they improve their ability to wait their turn and remain in control of their actions. Consider pointing out to children that they are good at remaining patient or that they can stop themselves from doing something they really want to do but should not do. When children know that these are desirable skills, they are more likely to use the skill during other parts of their day.

The following games and activities will help children improve their inhibitory-control skills.

Activity: What Should He Do?

In this example, children follow along with Danny, a superhero-in-training in the book *What Should Danny Do?* by Adir Levy. This is a choose-your-own-adventure book that features Danny, a little boy who has big choices to make. Children get to pick Danny's choices, most of which are related to inhibitory control and patience. They learn the consequences of Danny's choices and the importance of self-control.

Intended Outcomes

- Children will improve active-listening skills.
- Children will learn about self-control.

Materials

What Should Danny Do? by Adir Levy

What to Do

1. Gather children in either a small or large group. This game works well with both sizes as either a center or a circle-time activity.
2. Read *What Should Danny Do?*
3. When Danny is faced with a choice, decide as a group what he should do and turn to the corresponding page in the book.
4. After reading the consequence of Danny's choice, talk about whether or not he made a good choice.
5. Continue reading the book, or go back to the previous page and see what happens when Danny makes the other choice.
6. At the end of the book, discuss Danny's choices, self-control, and patience.
7. If time allows, discuss scenarios similar to Danny's, and ask the children what they would do in those situations.

Activity: Classroom Red Light, Green Light

Classroom Red Light, Green Light is similar to the familiar game Red Light, Green Light. In this version, instead of running when the light is green and stopping when it is red, children engage in seated activities. When the teacher calls out, "Green light," children do the activity. When the teacher calls out, "Red light," children must stop what they are doing and wait patiently to hear "green light." This activity directly targets inhibitory-control skills because children may only work on the activity when they hear "green light." Likewise, when they hear "red light," the children must inhibit their desire to begin working again.

Intended Outcomes

- Children will improve self-control skills.
- Children will inhibit their desire to do something when it isn't the right time.
- Children will improve active-listening skills.

Materials

Timer
Green light visual (optional)
Red light visual (optional)

Remaining materials will vary based on the activity. Choose a classroom activity that is repetitive in nature, such as coloring, gluing colorful ripped paper pieces onto cardboard or cardstock, stacking blocks, or sorting manipulatives.

What to Do

1. Tell the children that the purpose of this game is to see how much work they can get done in the allotted time. Tell them also that they must stop working when someone calls "red light" and cannot resume working until someone calls "green light."
2. Hand out the activity materials, such as a coloring page and crayons.

3. Tell the children, "Red light"—they must wait to start. Then call out, "Green light," and let them work on the activity for a minute.
4. Call out "Red light" to tell them to stop.
5. Play the game for several minutes, calling out "Green light" and "Red light" periodically.
6. When the rounds are over, talk with the children about how they feel about their finished product, how they felt when they had to wait and do nothing, and how they felt when a green light allowed them to work.
7. If time permits, play the game again, either continuing with the same activity or starting a new one.

Children can apply the concept they learn while playing Red Light, Green Light throughout the school day. For example, if the teacher needs to make a special announcement while children are engaged in centers or free play, the teacher may call out "red light," cueing children to stop whatever they are doing. The teacher makes the announcement and then calls out "green light," cueing children to go back to what they were doing.

Activity: Freeze Dance

Freeze dance is another activity that directly targets inhibitory-control skills because children may only dance when the music is on. When the music shuts off, they must stop dancing and try to freeze in place. Children who are unable to freeze and maintain their pose are called out and must sit down. The last child standing wins the round.

Intended Outcomes

- Children will work on active-listening skills.
- Children will improve self-control skills.
- Children will learn to inhibit their desire to do something when it isn't the right time.
- Children will engage in movement input.

Materials

Music that can easily be turned on and off

What to Do

1. Gather the children as a whole group, making sure everyone has enough space to safely move around.
2. Explain the rules of the game:
    - Children will dance or move their bodies when the music is turned on.
    - When the music is turned off, children must stop and freeze in place.
    - Any child who moves while the music is turned off must sit down until the round has finished.
3. Answer any questions.
4. Begin the game by turning on the music.
5. Continue to turn the music on and off until only one child is left.
6. Play again if the game finishes quickly and there is time.

To add variety to this game, consider music with different tempos. Fast and lively music may produce fast and lively dancing. Music with a slower beat may produce movements that are slower and more rhythmic.

Putting It All Together

This chapter offers ideas for classroom games and activities to help strengthen children's executive-function skills. The next chapter focuses on how to apply strategies to teach children to use their executive-function skills throughout the day.

Chapter 7:

Supporting Executive-Function Skills throughout the Day

The previous four chapters describe specific play, sensory, and cognitive games, activities, and strategies to improve children's executive-function skills. This chapter explains how to embed these into the classroom routine to support children's attentional flexibility, working memory, and inhibitory control. Supporting executive-function skills throughout the day will help children remember what they need to, complete activities in a timely manner, and engage in what they should be doing.

Supporting Attentional Flexibility throughout the Day

Supporting attentional flexibility in early learning classrooms helps children remain flexible and respond to changes and disruptions to the classroom routine. Often, a school day is filled with situations out of students' control that disrupt the typical routine, such as classmates breaking the rules or items going missing. Strong attentional-flexibility skills are important so that students can accept these events. The more children are exposed to thinking and acting in flexible ways, the better they will be at accessing strategies to remain flexible when they need to be. The following are common strategies that you can use throughout the day to support attentional flexibility.

Support Development of Theory of Mind

Young children are just starting to learn how they feel about certain things, so the idea that someone else may feel differently from them (called theory of mind) may not be something they grasp yet (Kimhi et al., 2014). Talking with children about another person's point of view will help them start to learn that people think and act in ways that may differ from their own thoughts and actions. This understanding supports attentional flexibility. By the end of kindergarten, many children will have developed an understanding of their own thoughts and feelings that will enable them to see that others may think and act differently.

Circle time is an excellent time in the day to engage in activities to support theory of mind. Choose and read books with strong characters to the class, pausing throughout the story to talk about why someone in the story acts the way they do. Encourage children to predict what a character might do next. These types of discussions will help young children gain insight into the thoughts and actions of others.

Model Flexible Thinking

Throughout the day, teachers and aides can model how they remind themselves to be flexible thinkers. When something comes up that requires a shift in thinking, trying something new, or engaging in an activity a different way, teachers can model how they adjust their thinking by talking out loud to the class about their thoughts and actions.

> Mr. Robert asked a local children's author to visit the class and read one of her stories. On the morning she was supposed to come in, the author woke up not feeling well and had to cancel. Mr. Robert shared this news with the class: "Today, we were going to have a special guest come into the classroom to read to us. But, our guest is sick and won't make it in. I'm disappointed that she can't come, but I hope she feels better soon. I'm going to choose a really great book, and I will read to the class instead."

Mr. Robert models flexible thinking for the class by explaining the change in routine, acknowledging his disappointment, and then offering a solution. By talking about changes and disruptions when they occur and then demonstrating how to deal with them, teachers can model flexible thinking and give children a strategy they can try the next time something happens that requires a shift in thinking or acting.

> Construction of a new playground structure for Falcon's Nest Elementary School's prekindergarten program was just completed. Ms. Sarah's pre-K class has been looking forward to playing outside on the new playground structure all week. As the class prepares to go outside, they hear an announcement that recess will be held indoors due to inclement weather. The children in Ms. Sarah's class erupt in disappointment. Ms. Sarah quickly gains the children's attention and says, "I am so sad that we've been looking forward to this day all week and now we can't go outside because it's raining. We can't control the weather, but we can control what we do with our time right now!" She pauses and smiles widely. "Let's go to the gym and play some games! We can play outside on the play structure tomorrow!" Ms. Sarah declares.

Ms. Sarah models flexible thinking for her class by showing them how to identify feelings and accept that they will not get to do what they expected to do and by offering an alternative activity to pass the time.

Play Red Light, Green Light

This game, described in detail in chapter 6, can be modified and used throughout the school day as a simple and effective way to help children know when they should work and when they should stop or pause. By employing the concept that a green light means it is time to work and a red light means it is time to stop or pause the activity, teachers can cue children to stop working during an important announcement or for a transition. Similarly, if children begin to lose interest in an activity or abandon what they are doing, teachers may point out that it is still green-light time so they should keep working. Once the children learn this activity, you can use it at any time during the day.

Ask "Can We Do It a Different Way?"

Teachers can utilize this activity, described in detail in chapter 6, throughout the school day to discuss changes to the routine or to help resolve inflexible thinking and conflict.

> The children in Mr. Marcus's kindergarten class really enjoy painting at the easel. However, the activity tends to be difficult for children to transition away from in a timely manner. When they return from winter break, the children notice that the easel has been removed from the classroom. Many ask Mr. Marcus where it has gone, stating that it is one of their favorite things to do at school. Mr. Marcus gathers the class and states, "I know many of you really like painting at the easel, but that isn't an option for the class anymore." After pausing and allowing children time to process this, he says, "There are lots of ways to paint and create art, though. Can we think of a different way?" He reminds the children that one of the center choices involves shaving cream, paint, and marbles. He also suggests fingerpainting and watercolors. Then, he asks the class for their thoughts.

In this example, Mr. Marcus has acknowledged that the children enjoy painting. Using the game "Can We Do It a Different Way?" he has allowed them the opportunity to think about new ways to create art, linking their enjoyment of painting at the easel with the flexibility to engage in a new art activity.

> Two children in Ms. Paula's pre-K class are constructing with blocks and magnetic tiles. They become upset when they cannot build a tower like they did the day before because some of the pieces are missing. Ms. Paula sits down with the children and asks them to explain to her what's going on. Clearly frustrated, they describe their dilemma. Ms. Paula begins to build with the tiles and asks, "How can you build something a different way using the pieces that you do have?"

Rather than remaining stuck on thinking about the pieces they don't have or the tower they want to build, Ms. Paula encourages the children to think about how they could build a different way from yesterday. She challenges them to get creative and build something different with the available materials.

Supporting Attentional Flexibility during the Classroom Routine

Certain times in classroom routines can be particularly challenging for children when they are asked to switch focus from one task or activity to another. This section details how these particular times—including transitions, changes in the usual routine, center time, circle time, and recess and outdoor time—give teachers lots of opportunities to help children strengthen their attentional flexibility.

Transitions

Young children will struggle with transitions from time to time, so it is important to support attentional flexibility in those moments. Some may have trouble getting started with an activity and then, once they do, may have trouble stopping. Others may become so engrossed in the activity that they can't stop. For example, Micah, a four-and-a-half-year-old prekindergarten student, loves arts and crafts. He spends a lot of time planning what he will make, leaving little time to actually work. Micah often becomes upset when art and craft time ends and usually refuses to clean up, exclaiming, "But I'm not done!" Consistently using transition supports throughout the school day will help children change gears more quickly and easily.

Most strategies that help with attentional flexibility during transitions also aid in time management. For example, auditory aids such as a bell or chime to signify that there are a few minutes left can be helpful. Playing or singing songs can help with cleanup. Visual aids such as a visual timer to show time passing until the activity ends, sand timers that show when there are five minutes or one minute left, and a class schedule posted in a spot that is easy for children to reference can help children manage their time.

Changes in the Usual Routine

One of the most important components of attentional flexibility is the ability to sustain attention on a relevant task while also remaining flexible about changes that occur, such as a fire drill, a bout of nausea, or a spilled drink. A change in a young child's usual routine can be hard for them to tolerate.

> One afternoon, Antonio's mom came early to pick up Antonio for a dentist appointment. He knew that he was going to be picked up early, but he didn't realize that he would miss DEAR (drop everything and read) time, which was his favorite part of the school day. When Ms. Carpenter, the classroom teacher, let Antonio know that it was time to pack up his things and go with his mom, Antonio acted as if he didn't hear her and continued to read his book. Antonio's mom then cued him that they needed to leave so they wouldn't be late for their appointment. Antonio became upset and disrupted the rest of the class as he cried and yelled about not wanting to leave.

While this behavior is understandable, it is important that children learn strategies to tolerate change as best they can. Strategies that support attentional flexibility when there is a change in the usual routine include the following:

- Warn children about change as soon as possible so they have time to process and understand the change.
- Continue to remind children about the change that will happen and talk about how this change makes people feel.
- Practice disruptions to the usual routine as an activity so that children learn strategies to cope with change.

Center Time

Center time can be challenging for young children. They may struggle to use attentional-flexibility skills because there is less adult support and more social interaction with same-aged peers in centers. This is a time when students will think and act differently from one another. It is also when they are encouraged to be problem-solvers, collaborators, and creative thinkers as they learn and explore materials with their peers. Students need strong attentional-flexibility skills to tolerate these situations.

Children who are inflexible in their thinking may become upset if they don't know how to engage with center activities without specific steps or rules. These children will benefit from prompts, visual models, and suggestions to help them get started with an open-ended, child-led center activity. They may also need reminders that, as long as no classroom rules are broken, there is no right or wrong way to use center materials. Some young children believe there is a right and wrong way to engage with materials. These children may cry, tell on friends, and argue during activities when they perceive that another child "isn't doing it right."

Strategies that help students access and use attentional flexibility include supporting theory-of-mind understanding, modeling flexible thinking, and engaging in thinking about how to do it a different way.

Circle Time

Circle time is typically when children can learn important attentional-flexibility strategies. It is an opportunity to model reactions to uncertainty, talk about problems and disruptions that have occurred in the school day, acknowledge changes to the usual routine, and compliment flexible thinkers.

Strategies to support and teach attentional flexibility during circle time include:

- Reading books with strong characters and discussing their feelings, thoughts, and actions

- Reading books in which things go wrong and discussing possible solutions
- Modeling flexibility
- Discussing situations in which flexible thinking is necessary
- Talking about problem solving or ways to do something differently when things go wrong
- Discussing common classroom conflicts and encouraging children to suggest solutions and alternate ideas

Recess and Outdoor Time

Recess is one of the least structured parts of the school day. It is a time when children may play how they want and with whomever they choose. Strong attentional-flexibility skills are required for outdoor play to be enjoyable and rewarding for children, as they are interacting primarily with their peers. Often, when conflicts arise, it is because sharing is necessary or a child doesn't like how another child is playing a game. Many children will need support to manage their frustration, wait their turn for a toy or an open swing, and handle conflict when it arises. Encourage flexible thinking with strategies including modeling, encouraging children to play in a different way, and choosing a different game or activity when resources are limited.

Supporting Working-Memory Skills throughout the School Day

Supporting working-memory skills throughout the school day will help children succeed in novel activities and social interactions. In the classroom, working memory helps children remember what they need to be paying attention to and use that information to complete tasks and activities. Because children can access new information stored in their brains as working memory for only a limited amount of time, it is important to teach new information right before children will use it.

The following strategies will help support and strengthen working-memory skills throughout the day:

- Support memorization of rules and routines
- Teach metacognition
- Use visual supports
- Encourage parroting
- Provide movement input
- Offer rhythmic proprioception input

Support Memorization of Rules and Routines

There are limits to the amount of information that a child's brain can store as working memory at one time. While this varies from child to child, no one has infinite capacity to store information and use it in working memory. One way to support working memory is by helping children memorize the classroom rules and routines. Practicing rules, routines, and activities that occur frequently allows children to commit the required steps to long-term memory. When children have memorized classroom rules and routines, they have more capacity in their working-memory center to retain new information.

At the start of the school year, and then regularly throughout the year, teach classroom rules, routines, and schedules. Teach and practice everyday routines, such as handwashing, transitioning from home to school, and cleaning up until the children understand and memorize them. It is also a good idea to post visuals to help children remember all of these things.

Teach Metacognition

When children learn to be aware of what they are (or should be) thinking about, they can begin to understand how they think and learn; what things are easy for them; and what challenges they may have with thinking, remembering, or learning.

Throughout the school day, but especially before novel activities, bring attention to the fact that remembering is important. Before teaching a new activity, talk with children about how they might think about and focus on the things they need to do so they complete activities to the best of their ability. As an effective metacognition strategy, provide them with a verbal cue: "Okay, now we are going to learn something new. We need to be listening with our ears, looking with our eyes, and remembering with our brains."

> Ms. Cohen, a preschool teacher, has created a set of visuals she uses to help children know what their senses are and how their senses are helpful in the classroom. She's printed out and laminated illustrations of an ear, an eye, and a brain. She's taught the class that ears are for listening, eyes are for looking and seeing, and the brain is for remembering. Each time she explains an activity to the class, she uses these visuals to cue the children that they should be listening to her directions, looking at what the activity is and what materials are needed, and remembering what to do.

Use Visual Supports

Visual supports are excellent ways to support working-memory skills. Post visuals of the classroom rules and routines so children may easily reference them. Consider developing visual checklists for activities that outline the steps in the correct order. Reference a visual of an eye, an ear, and/or a brain when cueing children that it is time to look, listen, and remember.

Encourage Parroting

Another effective strategy that supports working-memory skills throughout the school day is to have students repeat novel instructions. Using age-appropriate language, give novel directions in small increments and then ask the class to repeat what they heard. They may parrot back the instructions in unison or explain the steps to a partner. Parroting helps remind children of what they should be remembering.

Once the class has repeated the instructions, encourage them to get started on the activity. Note that information stored in working memory does not stay there for very long. It is easy to forget the instructions if too much time passes between when the information is given and when it needs to be used.

Provide Movement Input

Providing movement input in two- to ten-minute intervals each hour throughout the day—especially before circle time and seated work—will support children's working-memory abilities because they will be more alert and active listeners. When children engage in movement input regularly throughout the school day, they are more focused and attentive during seated activities. Common movement inputs appropriate for the classroom include Freeze Dance, yoga, and calisthenic exercises, such as push-ups, sit-ups, running in place, and wall push-ups.

Offer Rhythmic Proprioception Input

Rhythmic proprioception inputs support working memory and attention. Pairing rhythmic input such as stomping or clapping with a prompt will support children's working memory so that they are better able to remember a sequence of events or directions to complete a task.

Rhythmic proprioception inputs include the following:

- Bouncing on a therapy ball
- Tapping the floor or their legs while seated
- Snapping fingers
- Clapping
- Jumping up and down in place

Encourage children to clap, tap, or jump as they recall and repeat the directions required to complete an activity. If they forget part of the instructions while engaged in the activity, remind them of the sequence of steps while clapping, snapping, or tapping.

Supporting Working Memory during the Classroom Routine

Center time, structured learning, and circle time provide teachers opportunities to support children's working memory.

Center Time

During center time, small groups of children engage in activities around the classroom. Typically, center activities are child led, which requires strong working-memory skills as they remember classroom rules and routines and encounter new information while they interact with different center-based activities. Embedding strategies that support working memory, such as the following, throughout learning blocks will help the children achieve their goals.

- Decrease visual distractions. A clutter-free classroom indirectly supports working memory, as children can attend to what they should rather than irrelevant things in the room.
- Design the classroom in a way that allows for easy movement from center to center.
- Use visuals to remind children what activities they can engage in at each center.
- Use visuals to remind children where tools and play objects belong.

Structured Learning

Structured learning time, or teacher-directed activities, are product driven. The teacher guides children through a goal-directed activity that has one outcome. Structured learning is important in kindergarten and some prekindergarten classrooms because it is an effective way to ensure that children are learning the content that they are focused on. As the teacher guides them through the learning module, they must draw on working-memory skills to listen to, remember, and then use information to complete the activity. Given that this type of learning tends to be highly structured, if the class has a low child-to-teacher ratio the children should be able to practice their working-memory skills while learning new activities with little difficulty. Strategies that help children access working memory during structured learning include:

- Teaching metacognition
- Providing visuals outlining the steps needed to complete the specific activity
- Offering movement input if attention wanes while children are seated

Circle Time

Circle time requires a lot of working memory. In large-group instruction, children need strong active-listening skills to focus and pay attention to what they need to, commit the information to memory, and hold this information in their minds while transitioning from circle time to the next activity. To best support working-memory skills, consider running circle time similarly each day. Maintaining a consistent circle-time routine will help children know what to expect. For example, an effective circle-time routine for three- to six-year-olds can be structured in the following way:

- Begin with an active-listening activity (1–3 minutes). This will help transition students to large-group learning. Active-listening activities might include:
    - hitting a small gong or ringing a bell. Children listen for the sound until they can no longer hear it.
    - singing a good-morning song.
    - hitting a small drum in an easy-to-follow rhythm that children copy by clapping or tapping their legs.
- Engage the class in a learning activity (3–5 minutes). The material may follow a theme the class has been learning about, such as rain forests or transportation, or it might be a discussion of the weather. Including a manipulative that matches the learning module will help children remain actively engaged in the activity. For example, if the class is learning about transportation, pass around a unique toy car or airplane.

- After a seated activity, consider a short, guided movement break (1–3 minutes). Guided movement such as Freeze Dance or yoga poses will give children controlled movement input that helps them remain alert and attentive to the rest of circle time.
- Read a story (3–10 minutes). The length of time for this activity will vary based on the children's attention span and age. Younger children may be able to sit and listen to a story for only three minutes; kindergarten children can remain attentive for up to ten minutes. However, there will be days when preschoolers can listen for longer than three minutes and the kindergarten class just doesn't have the attention skills to sit for more than a brief period. Remaining flexible and recognizing these nuances ensures a successful circle-time experience.
- Engage children in a closing song and/or give them transition information (3–5 minutes). If the children are learning novel instructions for an upcoming activity, cue them that it is time to really listen and remember what you are about to say. Share the information in small chunks using age-appropriate language. Encourage the children to repeat what they just heard to help them remember all of the information.

Teaching and Using Inhibitory Control throughout the Day

Supporting children's use of their inhibitory-control skills—attentional inhibition and response inhibition in particular—throughout the day helps them do what they should be doing. Children must continually inhibit their attention to irrelevant visual and auditory distractions happening all around them so that they are able to attend to what they should. Whether it is a child talking, a person walking in the hallway, or a bird chirping outside, distracting inputs occur all day long. A primary way to support attentional inhibition throughout the day is to reduce the visual and auditory distractions in the classroom environment. When the environment is filled with distractions, children tend to be distracted.

Create a classroom that is easy to navigate, has consistent furniture placement, and is clutter-free and quiet. Strategies to support attentional inhibition include using movement input to support active-listening skills and adding multisensory learning supports.

Most young children struggle with response inhibition. Children may push to the front of the line because they want to be first. They might blurt out an answer when it isn't their turn. They might push or act aggressively with their peers rather than use their words to talk through a situation. Each of these examples indicates a lack of strong response-inhibition skills, which is developmentally appropriate for preschool through early kindergarten. Because they are still learning how to be patient and maintain self-control, treating response inhibition like a skill that needs to be learned will help them follow the rules and routines of the classroom. By developing response-inhibition skills through modeling and metacognition activities, children can remain calm, patient, and in control of their responses. Strategies to teach and support response inhibition include using movement input during seated activities, cueing metacognition strategies, and modeling theory-of-mind skills.

Use Movement Input

Movement can help children transition from one activity to another. When children consistently engage in movement activities, they often store up that input and access it later during seated activities. Providing opportunities to move, work on balance, or hold yoga poses throughout the school day supports attentional and response inhibition, as children will be better able to sit for longer periods and concentrate on the tasks at hand. Children who crave movement input but don't get enough of it tend to move their bodies inappropriately rather than focus on what they should. To support attention during seated learning and mealtimes, consider adding two to four minutes of movement input before children transition to the activity. Effective movement inputs include:

- Yoga poses
- Freeze Dance

- Follow the Leader
- Hopping or jumping in place

Add Multisensory Learning Supports

Adding visual, auditory, and/or tactile sensory supports to seated activities will increase children's interest level, thereby indirectly supporting their attentional inhibition. When learning activities incorporate multisensory components, children tend to be more engaged and attentive. For example, listening to the teacher talk about the rain forest while looking at photos or books and interacting with objects found in the rain forest (plastic bugs, brightly colored toy birds, and so on) will more effectively encourage active listening and learning than words alone.

Multisensory supports might include items children can touch and hold as well as visuals of lesson items children can see while listening to a lesson.

Cue Metacognition Strategies

Before an activity, metacognition strategies cue children to think about how good they are at paying attention, waiting their turn, and keeping their hands to themselves. Such strategies make them aware of how they maintain self-control. Cueing children before an activity that they will need to look, listen, and remember helps them become mindful of how they learn and that they have control over their attention, focus, and self-control.

Model Theory-of-Mind Skills

Theory of mind can help children develop inhibitory control in the classroom environment. When they are able to think about another person's point of view, they can see how their actions might affect that person. For example, over time, children learn that taking a toy from a friend simply because they want it hurts the other child's feelings, or that blurting out an answer rather than waiting their turn frustrates other children. Read books with characters who break the rules and make decisions that have an effect on the people around them. Talk with children about how they think the characters in the book feel and how their actions affect others, encouraging them to share their ideas about what the characters could do differently next time.

Supporting Inhibitory Control during the Classroom Routine

Children's ability to focus on what is relevant while suppressing their attention to everything else will help them succeed during circle time and center time. This section reviews strategies teachers can use to support children's inhibitory control during these particular times of the daily routine.

Circle Time

Children need strong inhibitory control to be successful during circle time. They need to inhibit their desire to blurt out answers, stand or walk around, and be distracted by everything else going on around them. Strategies that help children with inhibitory control during circle time include using movement input, adding multisensory input, and modeling metacognition.

Movement games that require children to actively listen during circle time will help with attention and focus and also teach inhibitory-control skills. Play a movement game such as Simon Says or Freeze Dance either at the beginning of circle time or in the middle of circle time.

When teaching a lesson during circle time, incorporate toys, books, and other items that support the lesson plan. This multisensory approach will support attentional inhibition. When children see an item and interact with it, they are more attentive to what they are learning. When they are passive participants, their attention may wander, and they may struggle with inhibitory control.

Circle time is an excellent opportunity to teach metacognition and theory-of-mind skills by role-playing or reading books. Choose a role-play activity or book with scenarios in which likable characters break the rules. Spend time talking about what happened, and predict what might happen next. Encourage children to think about how each character feels, what happened when the character broke the rules, or what the character could have done instead.

Center Time

Children need strong inhibitory-control skills to manage their impulses and attend to what they should while engaging with their peers during center activities. Because center time is child led, children will benefit from external strategies to support both their attention and response-inhibition skills. Strategies that support inhibitory-control skills during center time include:

- Maintaining a consistent classroom design that is free of clutter and distractions
- Cleaning up toys, games, and activities so that center areas are free from external distractions
- Providing visuals of classroom rules and routines
- Providing visual timers or sand timers to help with time management

A Final Note

Attentional flexibility, working memory, and inhibitory control are skills that children need time to learn, support to develop, and opportunities to practice so that they are as successful as possible throughout the day. Embedding the strategies and activities from this book into your classroom routine will set children on the path to success. Refer to *Organized and Engaged* often to help all children in your classroom develop and improve their executive-function skills so they can become the best students they can be.

Glossary of Terms

arousal level: refers to how awake and alert a person is

attentional flexibility: the ability to switch focus from one person, task, or activity to another in response to a change in the situation. It is responsible for skills including filtering, task switching, and flexible thinking.

attentional inhibition: a type of inhibitory control; the ability to block out irrelevant information such as visual and auditory distractions and focus on what matters. It is the brain's ability to focus on something important while tuning out other visual and auditory stimuli.

chunking: the process by which children who have experience with an activity remember some or all of the steps necessary to complete it. When an activity is novel, each step will need to hold a place in a child's working memory.

co-regulation: Self-regulation develops in part due to the interactions children have with their caregivers, including their teachers while they are at school. Co-regulation happens when caregivers and familiar adults help children understand and process the many emotions they are experiencing at the moment, calming them down when they become upset.

executive function: a group of mental skills that includes attentional flexibility, working memory, and inhibitory control. Children rely on these three executive-functions skills to learn, play, and socialize throughout the school day.

filtering: the ability to recognize the difference between important and irrelevant information

flexible thinking: a skill that helps people look at situations in different ways, find new solutions to solve problems, and shift gears when what is supposed to happen doesn't

inhibitory control: the ability to stop and think before reacting. This is responsible for repressing inappropriate thoughts or actions and responding in a way that matches the task, activity, or social situation. It is also responsible for the ability to tune out the unimportant things going on in the environment to focus on what is relevant.

metacognition: the awareness of one's thought process; it refers to how people think about the way they think

pretend play: when children copy the actions of a familiar job or scenario, such as playing house, school, or restaurant

proprioception: the way the body senses movement and understands how to move through space. It is responsible for motor-planning movements, such as picking up a glass of water, drinking from it, and putting it back down again without spilling anything. It is also responsible for being able to walk through the classroom without bumping into things.

role-play: when a child or group of children pretend to be another person or character. For example, a child may switch roles with the classroom teacher.

response inhibition: a type of inhibitory control; the ability to stop and think before acting

self-regulation: the ability to remain calm and in control of oneself when faced with big emotions

sensory play: an activity that stimulates the senses—vestibular, proprioception, touch, sight, hearing, smell, and taste

stereognosis: the ability to perceive a shape or form using only the sense of touch

task switching: the unconscious shifting of attention from one activity to another. It also refers to the ability to switch the requirements of a task based on changing rules and requirements.

theory of mind: a person's ability to think about how someone else thinks. Specifically, it is the understanding that other people may have different thoughts and beliefs about something that may cause them to feel and act differently. Theory of mind is important for succeeding in social interactions, understanding and following rules, and achieving attentional flexibility.

vestibular sense: responsible for balance and how the body interprets and responds to movement

working memory: a type of short-term memory that helps people hold onto important information long enough to use it. It is the small amount of important information children need to successfully engage in immediate cognitive tasks, elaborate play, and social interactions.

References and Recommended Readings

Ahmed, Sammy F., et al. 2022. "Working Memory Development from Early Childhood to Adolescence Using Two Nationally Representative Samples." *Developmental Psychology* 58(10): 1962–1973.

American Academy of Pediatrics, American Public Health Association, National Resource Center for Health and Safety in Child Care and Early Education. 2011. *Caring for Our Children: National Health and Safety Performance Standards: Guidelines for Early Care and Education Programs*. 3rd edition. Elk Grove Village, IL: American Academy of Pediatrics.

Anderson, Peter. 2002. "Assessment and Development of Executive Function (EF) During Childhood." *Child Neuropsychology* 8(2): 71–82.

Anderson, Vicki A., et al. 2001. "Development of Executive Functions Through Late Childhood and Adolescence in an Australian Sample." *Developmental Neuropsychology* 20(1): 385–406.

Anzman-Frasca, Stephanie, Lori A. Francis, and Leann L. Birch. 2015. "Inhibitory Control is Associated with Psychosocial, Cognitive, and Weight Outcomes in a Longitudinal Sample of Girls." *Translational Issues in Psychological Science* 1(3): 203–216.

Austin Gina, Karoline Groppe, and Birgit Elsner. 2014. "The Reciprocal Relationship Between Executive Function and Theory of Mind in Middle Childhood: A 1-Year Longitudinal Perspective." *Frontiers in Psychology* 5(655).

Ayres, A. Jean. 1972. *Sensory Integration and Learning Disorders*. Los Angeles: Western Psychological Services.

Barkley, Russell A. 2010. "Differential Diagnosis of Adults with ADHD: The Role of Executive Function and Self-Regulation." *The Journal of Clinical Psychiatry* 71(7): e17.

Boyce, Peter, et al. 2006. "Lighting Quality and Office Work: Two Field Simulation Experiments." *Lighting Research and Technology* 38(3): 191–233.

Bundy, Anita C., Shelly J. Lane, and Elizabeth A. Murray. 2002. *Sensory Integration: Theory and Practice*. 2nd edition. Philadelphia, PA: F. A. Davis.

Chen, Hsin-Yung, Hsiang Yang, H.-J. Chi, H.-M. Chen. 2013. "Physiological Effects of Deep Touch Pressure on Anxiety Alleviation: The Weighted Blanket Approach." *Journal of Medical and Biological Engineering* 33(5): 463–470.

Chu, Claudia P-K. 2021. "Can 'Theory of Mind' Be Taught in School?" *Cambridge Educational Research e-Journal* 8: 63–79.

Cowan, Nelson. 2013. "Working Memory Underpins Cognitive Development, Learning, and Education." *Educational Psychology Review* 26(2): 197–223.

Diamond, Adele. 2002. "Normal Development of Prefrontal Cortex from Birth to Young Adulthood: Cognitive Functions, Anatomy, and Biochemistry." In *Principles of Frontal Lobe Function*. London, England: Oxford University Press.

Diamond, Adele, and Kathleen Lee. 2011. "Interventions Shown to Aid Executive Function Development in Children 4 to 12 Years Old." *Science* 333(6045): 959–964.

Dowsett, Sharon M., and David J. Livesey. 2000. "The Development of Inhibitory Control in Preschool Children: Effects of 'Executive Skills' Training." *Developmental Psychobiology* 36(2): 161–174.

Hofmann, Wilhelm, Brandon J. Schmeichel, and Alan D. Baddeley. 2012. "Executive Functions and Self-Regulation." *Trends in Cognitive Sciences* 16(3): 174–180.

Howard, Steven J., and Elena Vasseleu. 2020. "Self-Regulation and Executive Function Longitudinally Predict Advanced Learning in Preschool." *Frontiers in Psychology* 11: 49. doi: 10.3389/fpsyg.2020.00049

Kimhi, Yael, et al. 2014. "Theory of Mind and Executive Function in Preschoolers with Typical Development versus Intellectually Able Preschoolers with Autism Spectrum Disorder." *Journal of Autism and Developmental Disorders* 44(9): 2341–2354.

Losinski, Mickey, Sara A. Sanders, Nicole M. Wiseman. 2016. "Examining the Use of Deep Touch Pressure to Improve the Educational Performance of Students with Disabilities: A Meta-Analysis." *Research and Practice for Persons with Severe Disabilities* 41(1): 3–18.

Lyons, Kristen, and Phillip D, Zelazo. 2011. "Monitoring, Metacognition, and Executive Function: Elucidating the Role of Self-Reflection in the Development of Self-Regulation. In *Advances in Child Development and Behavior.* Vol. 40. Cambridge, MA: Academic Press.

May-Benson, Teresa A., and Jane A. Koomar. 2010. "Systematic Review of the Research Evidence Examining the Effectiveness of Interventions Using a Sensory Integrative Approach for Children." *American Journal of Occupational Therapy* 64(3): 403–414.

McClelland Megan M., et al. 2013. "Relations between Preschool Attention Span-Persistence and Age 25 Educational Outcomes." *Early Childhood Research Quarterly* 28(2): 314–324.

Michel, Eva, and Antonia Bimmüller. 2023. "The Factorial Structure of Executive Functions in Kindergarten Children: An Explorative Study." *Child Neuropsychology* 29(6): 862–885.

Montroy, Janelle J., et al. 2016. "The Development of Self-Regulation Across Early Childhood." *Developmental Psychology* 52(11): 1744–1762.

Murray, Desiree W., Katie Rosanbalm, Christina Christopoulos, and Amar Hamoudi. 2014. "Self-Regulation and Toxic Stress: Foundations for Understanding Self-Regulation from an Applied Developmental Perspective." OPRE Report #2015-21. Washington, DC: Office of Planning, Research and Evaluation, Administration for Children and Families, U.S. Department of Health and Human Services.

Pediatric Therapy Network. 2003. *Applying Sensory Integration Principles Where Children Live, Learn, and Play*. DVD. Torrance, CA: Pediatric Therapy Network.

Schmeichel, Brandon J, Rachael N. Volokhov, and Heath A. Demaree. 2008. "Working Memory Capacity and the Self-Regulation of Emotional Expression and Experience." *Journal of Personality and Social Psychology* 95(6): 1526–1540.

Schmitt, Lauren M., Lisa D. Ankeny, John A. Sweeney, and Matthew M. Mosconi. 2016. "Inhibitory Control Processes and the Strategies That Support Them during Hand and Eye Movements." *Frontiers in Psychology* 7(1927).

Smith, Hayley, Alice S. Carter, Eric Blaser, and Zsuzsa Kaldy. 2019. "Successful Attentional Set-Shifting in 2-Year-Olds with and without Autism Spectrum Disorder." *PLoS One* 14(3): e0213903.

Smolders, Karin C. H. J., and Yvonne A. W. de Kort. 2013. "Bright Light and Mental Fatigue: Effects on Alertness, Vitality, Performance, and Physiological Arousal." *Journal of Environmental Psychology* 39: 77–91.

Stahl, Laura, and Rene Pry. 2005. "Attentional Flexibility and Perseveration: Developmental Aspects in Young Children." *Child Neuropsychology* 11(2): 175–189.

Tamm, Leanne, and Paul A. Nakonezny. 2015. "Metacognitive Executive Function Training for Young Children with ADHD: A Proof-of-Concept Study." *Attention Deficit and Hyperactivity Disorders* 7(3): 183–190.

Tarle, Stephanie J., R. Matt Anderson, Elaine F. Arrington, and Delanie K. Roberts. 2019. "Emotion Regulation and Children with Attention-Deficit/Hyperactivity Disorder: The Effect of Varying Phonological Working Memory Demands." *Journal of Attention Disorders* 25(6): 851–864.

van der Veer, Gerda, Marja H. Cantell, Alexander E. M. G. Minnaert, and Suzanne Houwen. 2022. "The Relationship between Motor Performance and Executive Functioning in Early Childhood: A Systematic Review on Motor Demands Embedded within Executive Function Tasks." *Applied Neuropsychology: Child* 1–22. doi: 10.1080/21622965.2022.2128675

Index

U

V

W